Film Piracy, Organized Crime, and Terrorism

Gregory F. Treverton, Carl Matthies, Karla J. Cunningham,
Jeremiah Goulka, Greg Ridgeway, Anny Wong

SAFETY AND JUSTICE PROGRAM and the
GLOBAL RISK AND SECURITY CENTER

This research was conducted jointly under the auspices of the Safety and Justice Program within RAND Infrastructure, Safety, and Environment and the RAND Center for Global Risk and Security, part of International Programs at RAND.

Library of Congress Cataloging-in-Publication Data

Film piracy, organized crime, and terrorism / Gregory F. Treverton ... [et al.].
    p. cm.
  Includes bibliographical references.
  ISBN 978-0-8330-4565-2 (pbk. : alk. paper)
    1. Organized crime—Social aspects. 2. Terrorism—Social aspects. 3. Video recordings—Pirated editions. 4. Product counterfeiting. 5. Piracy (Copyright) I. Treverton, Gregory F.

  HV6431.F554 2009
  364.16'68—dc22

                                             2008046084

The RAND Corporation is a nonprofit research organization providing objective analysis and effective solutions that address the challenges facing the public and private sectors around the world. RAND's publications do not necessarily reflect the opinions of its research clients and sponsors.

RAND® is a registered trademark.

Published 2009 by the RAND Corporation
1776 Main Street, P.O. Box 2138, Santa Monica, CA 90407-2138
1200 South Hayes Street, Arlington, VA 22202-5050
4570 Fifth Avenue, Suite 600, Pittsburgh, PA 15213-2665
RAND URL: http://www.rand.org/
To order RAND documents or to obtain additional information, contact
Distribution Services: Telephone: (310) 451-7002;
Fax: (310) 451-6915; Email: order@rand.org

Preface

This report presents the findings of research into the involvement of organized crime and terrorist groups in counterfeiting a wide range of products, from watches to automobile parts, from pharmaceuticals to computer software. It presents detailed case studies from around the globe in one area of counterfeiting, film piracy, to illustrate the broader problem of criminal—and perhaps terrorist—groups finding a new and not-much-discussed way of funding their nefarious activities. Although there is less evidence of involvement by terrorists, piracy is high in payoff and low in risk for both groups, often taking place under the radar of law enforcement.

The study was made possible by a grant from the Motion Picture Association (MPA). However, the views expressed herein are those of the authors and do not necessarily reflect the opinions of the MPA. To be sure, the MPA, like other industries afflicted by counterfeiting, has powerful interests in the assessments presented in this report. Those evident stakes required that the authors be especially careful in examining evidence and framing conclusions. The research was conducted and the findings validated independently under the joint auspices of the Center for Global Risk and Security, part of the RAND Corporation's National Security Research Division, and the Safety and Justice Program in RAND Infrastructure, Safety, and Environment.

The mission of RAND Infrastructure, Safety, and Environment is to improve the development, operation, use, and protection of society's essential physical assets and natural resources and to enhance the related social assets of safety and security of individuals in transit and in their workplaces and communities. Research in the Safety and Justice Program addresses issues of occupational safety, transportation safety, food safety, and public safety—including violence, policing, corrections, substance abuse, and public integrity. For more information on the program, contact Acting Director Gregory Ridgway. He can be reached by email at gregr@rand.org; by phone at 310-393-0411, extension 7734; or by mail at The RAND Corporation, 1776 Main Street, P.O. Box 2138, Santa Monica, California 90407-2138.

The new RAND Center for Global Risk and Security, part of International Programs at RAND, aims to improve public policy by providing decisionmakers and the public with rigorous, objective research on critical policy issues, especially on the "newer" dimensions of security, dimensions that cut across traditional categories such as strategy, technology, law enforcement, and civil justice. For more information on the RAND Center for Global Risk and Security, contact the Director, Gregory F. Treverton. He can be reached by email at gregt@rand.org; by phone at 310-393-0411, extension 7122; or by mail at The RAND Corporation, 1776 Main Street, P.O. Box 2138, Santa Monica, California 90407-2138. More information about RAND is available at www.rand.org.

Contents

Figures and Tables

Figures

Tables

Summary

- *In Italy, a former Mafia boss turned government witness outlined how the Camorra, at times working in cooperation with Chinese and Taiwanese triads, generated millions of dollars from counterfeiting, including film piracy.*
- *In Malaysia, the Ang Bin Hoey triad has engaged in turf battles to maintain control over lucrative piracy markets, battles that resulted in knife and spear fights; robberies of bystanders, including families at bus stops; and assassinations of rival gang leaders.*
- *In Britain, 21 illegal Chinese immigrants drowned in the rising tide of Morecambe Bay while harvesting shellfish at night in treacherous waters. The victims had been forced into servitude by a slavemaster whose accomplice was found to have 4,000 counterfeit DVDs, copiers, and other equipment used for film piracy.*
- *The tri-border area of Brazil, Argentina, and Paraguay has emerged as the most important financing center for Islamic terrorism outside the Middle East, channeling $20 million annually to Hezbollah. At least one transfer of $3.5 million was donated by known DVD pirate Assad Ahmad Barakat, who received a thank-you note from the Hezbollah leader. Barakat was labeled a "specially designated global terrorist" by the U.S. government in 2004.*
- *In Russia, pirate syndicates are routinely tipped off by corrupt police officials prior to raids and have been permitted to run their businesses on government property and even from prison. Organized-crime figures involved in piracy have been known to resort to violence against rivals. Alleged pirates Ayrat Sharipov and Yevgeny Ladik and anti-*

piracy investigators were murdered, and an attempt was made on the life of the head of the Russian Anti-Piracy Organization.

As these cases indicate, DVD piracy, which has a higher profit margin than narcotics and minimal risks of enforcement, is attractive around the world as an element of criminal portfolios that also include drugs, money laundering, extortion, and human smuggling. The 14 case studies in this report provide compelling evidence of a broad, geographically dispersed, and continuing connection between film piracy and organized crime.

Moreover, three of the documented cases provide clear evidence that terrorist groups have used the proceeds of film piracy to finance their activities. While caution must be exercised in drawing broad conclusions from limited evidence, further investigation is a timely imperative. These cases, combined with established evidence for the broader category of counterfeiting-terrorism connections, are highly suggestive that intellectual-property theft—a low-risk, high-profit enterprise—is attractive not only to organized crime, but also to terrorists, particularly opportunistic members of local terrorist cells.

Whether the ends are financial gain or terrorism, the means are the same. Counterfeiting is widely used to generate cash for diverse criminal organizations. In the case of DVD film piracy, criminal groups are moving to control the entire supply chain, from manufacture to distribution to street sales, consolidating power over this lucrative black market and building substantial wealth and influence in virtually every region of the globe. In some areas, this influence extends to law enforcement and political leaders, who are bought, intimidated, or induced to create "protected spaces" where crime flourishes.

Table S.1 summarizes the criminal groups examined in this report, their bases, and the range of crimes they commit.

The main difference between organized crime and terrorism is motivation—financial gain for the former and a political agenda for the latter. However, the motivations of a group's members can change over time in reaction to changed circumstances. For example, the Irish Republican Army (IRA), a terrorist group that once supported itself in part with the proceeds of crime, devolved into a criminal group, while

Table S.1
Criminal Groups, Bases, and Range of Criminal Activities

Organized-Crime Group	Base Location	Film Piracy	Counterfeiting	Racketeering	Human Smuggling	Money Laundering/ Illegal Money Transfer Service	Illegal Gambling	Loan-Sharking	Narcotics Trafficking	Prostitution	Weapon Trafficking	Contract Killing	Document Forgery Services
Big Circle Boys	Canada	x		x	x	x	x	x	x	x	x	x	x
Yi Ging	USA	x		x	x	x	x	x	x	x	x	x	
Jah organization	USA	x	x			x							x
Cockle-picker gangmaster	England	x	x		x								
Lotus Trading Company	England	x	x		x								
Madrid Human smuggling ring	Spain	x			x								x
Camorra Mafia	Italy	x	x	x	x	x	x	x	x	x	x	x	x
Wo Shing Wo triad	Hong Kong	x	x	x	x	x	x	x	x	x	x	x	x
San Yee On triad	Hong Kong	x	x	x	x	x	x	x	x	x	x	x	x
Ang Bin Hoey triad	Malaysia	x	x	x	x	x	x	x	x	x	x	x	x
Barakat network	Paraguay	x	x	x		x	x		x		X		x
PIRA/RIRA	N. Ireland	x	x	x							X		
UDA/UFF/UVF	N. Ireland	x	x	x					x		X		
D-Company	Pakistan	x	x	x		x			x		X	x	
Tarantsev/Orehovsko-Medvedkovsky	Russia	x	x			x						x	
Los Ambulantes/Tepito	Mexico	x	x	x		x	x		x	x	X		x
Yamaguchi-gumi/Yakuza	Japan	x	x	x	x	x	x		x	x	x	x	x

India's D-Company appears to have morphed from a traditional criminal syndicate motivated by money to a terrorist group motivated by a political agenda funded at least in part with the proceeds of crime. As set forth in this report, both the IRA and D-Company have used film piracy to help fund their activities.

The evidence assembled in this report testifies that counterfeiting is a threat not only to the global information economy, but also to public safety and national security. It represents a call to cooperation in the battle against intellectual-property theft for law enforcement and governments around the world. Five ingredients are critical to meaningful progress:

- Increased political will
- Strong legislation
- Consistent enforcement
- Deterrent sentencing
- Innovative solutions.

Increased Political Will. Governments worldwide should commit resources and establish high-level accountability for intellectual-property protections, adding organized crime and piracy to the agenda of influential global gatherings such as the G-8 and the Davos Economic Summit, conducting periodic legislative hearings and public-awareness campaigns, and sharing intelligence with industry-led anti-piracy efforts.

Strong Legislation. The legal definition of "organized crime" should be expanded to include large-scale counterfeiting tied to other criminal activity. Laws should be enacted to grant investigators greater authority to sustain investigations, conduct surveillance, and obtain search warrants.

Consistent Enforcement. Authorities should be provided with guidelines for ways to trace back up the production and distribution chain. This requires processing cases quickly to reduce the risk that informants will be intimidated, and it means enhancing international cooperation to mirror the borderless nature of criminal networks.

Deterrent Sentencing. The current light sentences for piracy provide neither deterrents to crime nor incentives to cooperate with authorities. That should change with increased understanding of the powerful links between piracy and organized crime. Key piracy cases should be fought in the organized-crime or money-laundering divisions of prosecutors' offices. Strong application of money-laundering and other statutes can work to reduce the financial appeal of these crimes. In addition, piracy should be made a priority offense within anti-gang strategies.

Innovative Solutions. Customs and immigration forms (and any enabling laws or regulations, if necessary) should be amended to include language prohibiting the importation of counterfeit goods. It is also important to enlist the financial community in spotting piracy syndicates' money-laundering tactics; to improve standards for transportation documents; and to increase public awareness of the consequences of intellectual-property theft. Governments should also consider making large-scale piracy an extraditable offense.

The exposure of the critical link between piracy and organized crime, along with an early-warning flag on terrorism, raises critical questions for policymakers and law enforcement about whether opportunities exist for pursuing piracy up the criminal food chain to uncover and perhaps prevent more-serious criminal acts. For example, in one case documented in this report, a simple arrest at a United Parcel Service (UPS) store for shipping illegal DVDs led to the exposure of a large-scale human-trafficking ring. There is a clear need for additional global intelligence gathering and sharing to further illuminate the scope and nature of the connections between piracy and organized crime. And the mandate is clear for policymakers and law enforcement around the world to revisit the common but erroneous assumption that counterfeiting is a victimless crime.

Acknowledgments

In taking on a project as challenging as this study, we incurred a number of intellectual debts, which we gratefully acknowledge. Our distinguished reviewers, Brian Jenkins and Phil Williams, combined rich perspectives on terrorism and organized crime, and their reviews pushed us to improve this report. Our colleagues at MPA—especially John Malcolm, Robert Bauer, and Rajiv Dalal—were interested and helpful, while always respectful of RAND's independence and objectivity. We would especially like to acknowledge the invaluable contributions of Jonathan Dotan, who gathered much of the primary-source evidence while serving as an organized-crime consultant to the MPA, then responded cheerfully to our repeated requests for more documentation.

CHAPTER ONE

Introduction: Defining the Issues

This report investigates the extent to which criminal and terrorist groups are engaging in counterfeiting, using film piracy as an example. It lays out a number of cases detailing the connections between organized criminal syndicates and counterfeiting and presents three case studies demonstrating the fact that some terrorist groups also engage in counterfeiting. It then explores the implications of that involvement and offers suggestions for ways in which both law enforcement and policy officials could address them.

This chapter defines the scope of the issues and outlines the research methods used here. The next chapter defines organized crime, terrorism, and piracy and describes the points of convergence and divergence between organized crime and terrorism. Probing those connections requires thinking beyond a static picture of current circumstances to consider how "organized crime" is itself changing and how the nature of terrorism is evolving or diversifying around the globe. Chapter Three turns to counterfeiting, using film piracy as an example of the low risks and high rewards that make this criminal activity so attractive. Chapters Four and Five offer detailed case studies of existing links between piracy and organized crime and between piracy and terrorism, respectively. Chapter Six uses cases to show that the money to be made from piracy can lead to corruption, which provides "protected spaces" in which crime is allowed to flourish. Chapters Seven and Eight present specific recommendations based on the study's findings. Finally, Appendixes A, B, and C (on the enclosed DVD) present the full details of the case studies.

The cases are presented in three overlapping categories. The first category demonstrates the involvement of organized crime in piracy; the second shows how three terrorist groups use piracy to fund their operations or benefit from its fruits even if they don't directly engage in it; and the third sets out the notion of "protected spaces" for piracy that are created when governments are too stretched, too complacent, or too corrupt to take serious actions against it. Several types of connections between organized crime and piracy and between terrorism and piracy are outlined, then mapped to the case studies. Those types form an organizing principle for the array of cases presented and also provide precision for answers to the analytical question of why groups expand into piracy. The cases are rich and are worth perusing in detail. But for the convenience of busy readers, each case begins with a bulleted summary of key points:

- **Highlight.** What is particularly salient or important about this case? What is the headline?
- **Piracy revenues.** How important is piracy in the criminal portfolio of the group involved?
- **Discovery of piracy.** When and how did the evidence of piracy arise? Did the group come to piracy from other crime, or did it begin with piracy?
- **Motivation for entry into piracy.** What was the type of connection between organized crime and film piracy, and between terrorism and film piracy?
- **Role of law enforcement.** What organization investigated the case? What charges were filed? What convictions were made?
- **Evidence base.** How compelling is the base of evidence on which the case rests?

The Scope of Counterfeiting

While concern over counterfeiting goes back to the Middle Ages, the past two decades have seen an explosion in the levels of counterfeiting and piracy within the global economy, in both the domestic and international arenas.[1] In today's sophisticated global economy—with its easy and widespread access to computers, copiers, scanners, and lightning-fast Internet access—there are virtually no product lines, corporations, or consumers that escape the reach of counterfeiters and/ or pirates. Never before has it been so easy to duplicate labels, packaging, documentation, authentication devices, and/or symbols, marks, and logos with such speed, accuracy, and relative anonymity.

The available numbers are estimates and should be taken with caution, but they do underscore a dramatic increase. By one estimate, "Trade in counterfeit goods has grown eight times faster than legitimate trade since the early 1990s."[2] In 1982, the U.S. International Trade Commission estimated losses to the United States from counterfeiting and piracy at $5.5 billion.[3] In 1988, losses were estimated at $60 billion.[4] In 1996, damage to the U.S. economy was estimated at $200 billion.[5] The U.S. Trade Representative (USTR) estimated losses

---

[1] The terms "piracy" and "counterfeiting" are used interchangeably in this report, although they can mean different things. Piracy might refer more narrowly to the act of stealing original intellectual property—in this case, movies—via online downloading or copying a legally produced optical disc; counterfeiting might more narrowly define the mass reproduction of optical discs for sale. We do not insist on this distinction here, because organized crime uses both piracy and counterfeiting to generate profit. We use piracy in a broader sense to refer to the entire process of theft, mass reproduction, and distribution.

[2] John R. Wagley, *Transnational Organized Crime: Principal Threats and U.S. Reponses*, Washington, D.C.: Congressional Research Service, CRS Report for Congress, RL33335, March 20, 2006, p. 5.

[3] See S. Rep. No. 104-177, 104th Cong., 1st Sess. 1-2 (1995). See also United States International Trade Commission, *The Effects of Foreign Product Counterfeiting on U.S. Industry*, Final Report on Investigation No. 332-158 Under Section 332(b) of the Tariff Act of 1930, USITC Publication 1479, pp. xiv and 24, January 1984.

[4] See United States International Trade Commission, *Foreign Protection of Intellectual Property Rights and the Effect on U.S. Industry and Trade*, Report to the United States Trade Representative, Investigation No. 332-245, Under Sec. 332(g) of the Tariff Act of 1930, USITC Publication 2065, App. H, February 1988.

[5] See S. Rep. No. 104-177, 104th Cong., 1st Sess. 1-2 (1995).

for 2005 in the same range, between $200 billion and $250 billion per year.[6]

While the world has perhaps been slow to realize it, it makes sense that organized crime would be involved in counterfeiting: The profit margins are huge, the cost of entry is minimal, and the risks are relatively low. Moreover, criminal groups can make use of infrastructure they have already developed for other purposes—to move people or drugs or money, for instance—for counterfeiting. Because much of counterfeiting has been dismissed as "victimless crime," just how lucrative it can be is unclear, as is the role of organized crime in this activity.

We do know that criminal groups are attracted to the money to be made, and counterfeiting becomes another part of their portfolio of illegal businesses—one that can both fund and be funded by other criminal ventures. In some cases, people smuggled illegally across national borders are forced to sell counterfeit goods in order to pay off some of the fees they owe their "coyotes" or "snakeheads"—persons or gangs involved in human smuggling—or have "accrued" to middlemen along the way. Selling counterfeit movies, for example, requires nothing more than the ability to say "three" or "four" or "five" in English (or another language).[7]

In testimony before the U.S. Congress in 2003, Ronald K. Noble, the Secretary General of Interpol, asserted: "The link between orga-

---

[6] United States Trade Representative, *2005 Special 301 Report*, April 2005. None of the sources are very clear about how the loss estimates were compiled, so those estimates should be treated as no more than suggestive. All dollars referred to in the report are U.S. dollars; sharp changes in exchange rates mean that any conversions from or to other currencies should be treated as only ballpark estimates.

[7] The Palermo conventions distinguish between *human smuggling*, in which people willingly pay to be moved illegally across borders, from *human trafficking*, in which coercion or deception is involved. In practice, the distinction can be fuzzy; the first can turn into the second as the people smuggled acquire additional debts along the way or are simply vulnerable to coercion. See *Crime Prevention and Criminal Justice: Report of the Ad Hoc Committee on the Elaboration of a Convention Against Transnational Organized Crime on the Work of Its First to Eleventh Sessions*, United Nations General Assembly, November 2, 2000, UNA/55/383. Available at http://www.uncjin.org/Documents/Conventions/dcatoc/final_documents/383e. pdf (as of September 12, 2008).

nized crime groups and counterfeit goods is well established. But Interpol is sounding the alarm that intellectual property crime is becoming the preferred method of funding for a number of terrorist groups."[8] The link between terrorism and counterfeiting as a means of funding, however, is not as definitive as the link between organized crime and counterfeiting. While skepticism is warranted about the role of organized crime in funding terrorism, evidence of three specific instances of a connection between film piracy and terrorism is detailed in Chapter Five. Moreover, connections between terrorism and the broader category of counterfeiting rest on an established base of evidence. In the early 1990s, for instance, the terrorists who led the first World Trade Center attack financed their operation through the sale of counterfeit T-shirts.[9]

One reason for skepticism is that terrorism is not very expensive. The best estimates put the cost of the September 11, 2001, attacks at about a half-million dollars and the costs of the first London attacks and the Madrid attacks well below that figure.[10] That is not to say that terrorists will not turn to crime, including counterfeiting, to finance their activities. In fact, they have frequently done so. It does imply, though, that terrorists may not engage in profit-generating criminal acts to the same extent that organized criminal syndicates do.

It is important to distinguish between criminal funding of terrorists by supporters and crimes by the terrorists themselves, and for the latter, between crime that is strategic and crime that is opportunistic on a cell-by-cell basis. In Northern Ireland, for instance, the piracy was strategic in the sense that groups on both sides that had engaged in ter-

---

[8] His prepared statement is available at http://www.interpol.int/Public/ICPO/speeches (as of September 12, 2008).

[9] Kathleen Millar, "Financing Terror: Profits from counterfeit goods pay for attacks," *U.S. Customs Today*, U.S. Customs, Office of Public Affairs, November 2002. Available at http://www.cbp.gov/xp/CustomsToday/2002/November/interpol.xml (as of September 12, 2008).

[10] United Nations Security Council, *First report of the Analytical Support and Sanctions Monitoring Team established pursuant to resolution 1526 (2004) concerning Al-Qaida and the Taliban and associated individuals and entities*, Richard Barrett, Coordinator (S/2004/679), July 31, 2004.

rorism used piracy to fund their activities and ultimately became, in effect, criminal organizations. In the tri-border area of South America, where Argentina, Brazil, and Paraguay meet, criminal sympathizers of Hezbollah were intricately involved in funneling the proceeds of counterfeiting to Hezbollah to fund its activities.

Terrorist groups need money, and they have shown themselves capable of moving into many illicit business lines to secure it. The cause may be used to justify any means, including criminality. According to one recent study of the Kurdish Workers' Party, "encouraging criminal activities 'is emerging as an integral feature of al-Qaeda's internal propaganda.'"[11] For their part, homegrown terrorists such as the Moroccan migrants who executed the Madrid bombings may start with connections to, or even come from, groups at the margins of society—another example of the blurring of what initially might seem a clear distinction between terrorism and organized crime. As terrorism studies expert Rohan Gunaratna puts it, "For present-day terrorist groups, criminal activities, especially low-level crime, have become a necessity. The trend reflects the speed and agility of cell-level terrorist operations and highlights just how difficult it is to monitor and take down these groups. Understanding this new frontier of terrorist financing is a critical task that requires new forms of cooperation and new modes of strategic thinking."[12]

Counterfeiting is often thought of as a "victimless crime." It is not. Quite apart from those who might lose their jobs when counterfeiters undercut their markets, people die every year from counterfeited pharmaceuticals, auto parts, baby formula, alcohol, and the like, which are sold with adulterated ingredients or inadequate safety inspections. According to the World Health Organization (WHO), counterfeit drugs account for 10 percent of all pharmaceuticals. That proportion

---

[11] Mitchel P. Roth and Murat Sever, "The Kurdish Workers Party (PKK) as Criminal Syndicate: Funding Terrorism through Organized Crime, A Case Study," *Studies in Conflict & Terrorism*, Vol. 30, No. 10, 2007, p. 904.

[12] Email from Rohan Kumar Gunaratna to Jonathan Dotan, September 24, 2008.

can rise to as high as 60 percent in developing countries.[13] According to WHO, 16 percent of counterfeit drugs contain the wrong ingredients, 17 percent contain incorrect amounts of the proper ingredients, and 60 percent have no active ingredients whatsoever.[14]

When a consumer is physically harmed by using a counterfeit product, the public is outraged and governments respond—striking examples include the appointment to head Nigeria's FDA-equivalent of Dr. Dora Akunyili, whose diabetic sister died in 1988 after taking counterfeit insulin, and the execution, in July 2007, of the director of the Chinese FDA-equivalent for gross corruption. However, when the victim of a crime is a brand owner or a movie studio, there is little or no outrage, even though the people who work in the affected industry have clearly suffered harm. Moreover, counterfeiting is obviously even more dangerous when nested with organized crimes of more serious sorts, not to mention deadly terrorist activities.

Note on Cases and Methods

This report draws on the first global, in-depth, on-site research that has produced case studies indicating the extent of the connections among organized crime, terrorism, and counterfeiting. In this study, some 2,000 pages of primary documents were analyzed, and interviews were conducted with more than 120 law enforcement and intelligence agents from more than 20 countries. Because of counterfeiting's image as a victimless crime and the fact that those who buy counterfeit goods are complicit in the crime, information about counterfeiting is sparse, and information about the involvement of organized crime is sparser still. Because most instances of counterfeiting go unaddressed, there is reason to believe that more-formal data, such as arrests and convictions, understate the extent of the crime.

---

[13] Helen Knight, "Fighting the Fakers," *The Engineer*, April 26, 2002, p. 16; Phillippe Broussard, "Dangerous Fakes," *World Press Review*, Vol. 44, No. 1, January 1999, p. 36.

[14] Douglas Pasternak, "Knockoffs on the Pharmacy Shelf: Counterfeit drugs are coming to America," *U.S. News & World Report*, June 11, 2001, p. 26.

In our investigation, we needed to be especially scrupulous about the methods we used and the language we employed. We began with the background of RAND's own work on terrorism, in particular, but also its research on crime and organized crime.[15] That body of work provided the context for assessing the specific case data that had been developed by the MPA, its affiliates around the world, and its consultants, often in cooperation with local police authorities. Much of the data from the MPA involves cases in the legal sense of the term—from raids and arrests to seizures, indictments, and convictions. The RAND team wrote up those cases in summary form and reviewed relevant documentation. The cases were then expanded (the full descriptions are presented in the Appendixes). They thus became case studies in the broader sense of the term—detailed looks at criminal or terrorists groups, their organizations, operations, and connections.

In some crucial areas, however—for example, China and Russia—on-site investigations are difficult or dangerous, or both, so we were compelled to rely more heavily on published accounts. Where possible, we sought both to add to that information and to cross-check it against RAND's own sources, including published case histories of organized crime rings, interviews with experts, and a wide variety of published accounts, including media reports. We then examined all the specific information within the broader context of understanding the evolving nature of organized crime, terrorism, and the roles of government. Finally, we subjected drafts of this report to rigorous quality control, both informal (comparing notes with the Federal Bureau of Investigation (FBI), the Central Intelligence Agency (CIA), police, and

---

[15] Recent examples include Angel Rabasa et al., *Beyond al-Qaeda: Part 1, The Global Jihadist Movement*, Santa Monica, CA: RAND Corporation, MG-429-AF, 2006; Angel Rabasa et al., *Beyond al-Qaeda: Part 2, The Outer Rings of the Terrorist Universe*, Santa Monica, CA: RAND Corporation, MG-430-AF, 2006; Brian A. Jackson et al., *Aptitude for Destruction: Volume 1, Organizational Learning in Terrorist Groups and Its Implications for Combating Terrorism*, Santa Monica, CA: RAND Corporation, MG-331-NIJ, 2005; Brian A. Jackson et al., *Breaching the Fortress Wall: Understanding Terrorist Efforts to Overcome Defensive Technologies*, Santa Monica, CA: RAND Corporation, MG-481-DHS, 2007; and Kim Cragin and Sara Daley, *Assessing the Dynamic Terrorist Threat*, Santa Monica, CA: RAND Corporation, RB-121-AF, 2004.

other interested analysts) and formal (detailed written reviews in the RAND Quality Assurance program).

Throughout this report, we try to be transparent about how confident we are in particular assertions or conclusions. In dealing with specific cases, we arrived at a kind of hierarchy of confidence. Because many of the cases involved some police action, the court and police records of arrests leading to convictions, especially in countries where justice is generally fair, are at the top of our hierarchy; next are police reports, where we also looked for corroborating sources or accounts, such as first-hand media accounts; and at the bottom of our confidence hierarchy are media accounts, which we treat and describe as only suggestive unless they are corroborated by other, independent accounts. In only a few instances, which we indicate, did we have to keep sources confidential to protect them from danger.

For secondary sources, we employed the same implicit scaling, looking at the sources cited by the work in question. For cases in several of the countries we examined, including Russia and Mexico, prosecution documents were rare or nonexistent; our purpose in examining those cases, though, was to understand the interaction of corruption, limited capacity, and the stakes of politicians, so the details of piracy crimes are less immediately pertinent.

CHAPTER TWO

Organized Crime and Terrorism

This chapter addresses organized crime and terrorism, how they can be defined, and how they are organized, and it outlines the global reach of the ills both cause. It outlines the similarities and the differences in the motivations of the two groups, and it looks at the variety of ways they find common cause despite the differences. A central common motivation is money: Organized crime seeks it, and terrorism needs it. This chapter explores the possibility that counterfeiting could become increasingly important to terrorists as terrorist groups become more cell-based, with more-obscure links to al Qaeda and other central organizations, and as the distinction blurs between crime intended to finance violence for political and ideological purposes and crime for money's sake.

Defining Organized Crime and Terrorism

There is no doubt that counterfeiting is a *crime,* but the first broader issue that arises in a world of globalization is that of defining *organized* crime. There is no statutory definition of organized crime in the United States, where it is legally referred to as "racketeering," with its many variants defined in the United States Code, Part 1, Chapter 95, § 1961. The most relevant of these definitions is in 18 U.S.C. 1961 1.b, which defines racketeering to be "any act which is indictable under any of the following provisions of title 18, United States Code: . . . section 2318 (relating to trafficking in counterfeit labels for phonorecords, computer programs or computer program documentation, or packaging and copies of motion pictures or other audiovisual works)."[1]

The canonical definition of organized crime comes from the FBI: "Any group having some manner of a formalized structure and whose primary objective is to obtain money through illegal activities. Such groups maintain their position through the use of actual or threatened violence, corrupt public officials, graft, or extortion, and generally have a significant impact on the people in their locales, region, or the country as a whole."[2]

This definition and others proposed by the United Nations and Interpol refer to individuals working in a structured organization to conduct criminal activities. The size of organized-crime groups can vary from a few people to several thousand. Their activities are executed to generate profits. In this sense, these groups are like business enterprises: They make rational choices about what "business" activities they engage in, whom they partner with, and how they manage their product lines and respond to market demands. The logic of the market, then, explains much criminal behavior and provides insights into the intersection of organized crime and terrorists or their supporters. What differentiates organized crime from legal business enterprises is that the "product" itself is illegal (drugs, prostitution, extortion), the goods are stolen (the stolen goods in counterfeiting consist of intellectual property), the business (smuggling of cigarettes or people) evades regulation, or the methods of protecting markets are illegal (protection by intimidation, threats, or actual violence).

Interestingly, the criteria for crime merge more easily into the definition of terrorism than the criteria for terrorism merge into the definition of crime. For example, the FBI defines terrorism as "the unlawful use of force and violence against persons or property to intimidate or coerce a government, the civilian population, or any segment thereof,

---

[1] Quoted in Jeffrey Scott McIllwain, "Intellectual Property Theft and Organized Crime: The Case of Film Piracy," *Trends in Organized Crime*, Vol. 8, No. 4, 2005, p. 18.

[2] Federal Bureau of Investigation, *Organized Crime*. Available at http://www.fbi.gov/hq/cid/orgcrime/glossary.htm (as of September 12, 2008).

in furtherance of political or social objectives." [3] And it defines organized crime as "use of actual or threatened violence, corrupt public officials, graft, or extortion, . . . generally [having] a significant impact on the people in their locales, region, or the country as a whole."

So, too, the United Nations Convention Against Transnational Organized Crime defines an organized criminal group as "a structured group of three or more persons, existing for a period of time and acting in concert with the aim of committing one or more serious crimes or offences established in accordance with this Convention, in order to obtain, directly or indirectly, a financial or other material benefit." [4] Notably, nothing is stated about the ultimate goals of the organization, only that a group functions together to obtain some form of financial and/or material benefit.

One useful distinction divides organized crime from sporadic crime. The former "involves enduring networks of actors engaged in ongoing and continuous money-raising activities," while the latter "involves individuals or (usually) small groups performing a one-off money-making criminal activity, or a series of more or less disconnected and intermittent actions/crimes." [5] A related distinction is that between a vertically integrated organization and a transaction-based supply chain or market. That is, does the criminal activity require a single enterprise, or can smaller groups engage in parts of the supply chain? Because counterfeiting requires some infrastructure, it does not lend itself to one-off crimes, yet because some forms of it, like DVD piracy, entail fairly low barriers to entry, smaller groups can, in principle, take on pieces of the criminal chain.

---

[3] Code of Federal Regulations, 28 C.F.R. Section 0.85. See U.S. Department of Justice, Federal Bureau of Investigation, *Terrorism 2000/2001*, FBI Publication 0308. Available at http://www.fbi.gov/publications/terror/terror2000_2001.htm (as of September 12, 2008).

[4] United Nations, *United Nations Convention Against Transnational Organized Crime*, 2000, p. 2. Available at http://www.uncjin.org/Documents/Conventions/dcatoc/final_documents_2/convention_eng.pdf (as of September 12, 2008).

[5] Steven Hutchinson and Pat O'Malley, "A Crime-Terror Nexus? Thinking on Some of the Links between Terrorism and Criminality," *Studies in Conflict & Terrorism*, Vol. 30, No. 12, 2007, pp. 7–8.

Indeed, the power of small groups in the global economy requires stretching the notion of "organized." That power derives from the confluence of technology, networks, and alliances. The FBI definition of organized crime still retains a tinge of the traditional Mafia about it: There is the suggestion of both geography and hierarchy in the groups. However, as a recent United Nations report states, "The traditional Mafia type organization—which is linked to its territory and which exercises pressing control by means of intimidation and extortion tactics—has gradually expanded to include new opportunities deriving from the globalization of markets and the widespread distribution of technologies."[6] Trade in narcotics and contraband products required a move away from hierarchy toward alliances with other groups across the globe. Crime became transnational. Moreover, with the coming of the digital age, information technology (IT) allows operations to shrink what IT specialists call the "minimum sustainable scale of operations." That is true for commerce, especially the huge "virtual" market of the Internet. It is also true for illicit commerce, perhaps especially for crimes where the barriers to entry are relatively low. Small groups can make major money—and cause major mayhem.

Differences Between Terrorism and Organized Crime

Terrorism is not very expensive, as has been emphasized. The Madrid train bombings of 2004 were first estimated to have cost as little as $10,000, though the later police investigations raised that number by a factor of at least five.[7] The bombing of the USS *Cole* in 2000 is esti-

---

[6] *Counterfeiting: A Global Spread, A Global Threat,* Report of the Anti-Human Trafficking and Emerging Crimes Unit of the United Nations Interregional Crime and Justice Research Institute (UNICRI), December 2007, p. 104.

[7] For the original estimate, see United Nations Security Council, *First Report of the United Nations Security Council Analytical Support and Sanctions Monitoring Team established pursuant to resolution 1526 (2004) concerning Al-Qaida and the Taliban and associated individuals and entities,* Richard Barrett, Coordinator (S/2004/679), 2004. The higher figure was the Spanish police estimate of between (euros) €41,000 and €54,000, as reported in *El País,* May 17, 2005.

mated to have cost as little as $5,000, while the London bombers of July 2005 may have spent only about $1,000.[8] Yet money is necessary, and beyond the funds needed to execute an attack, funds are also required to finance day-to-day recruiting, training, and maintenance, and to provide sanctuary for terrorist organizations.[9] Hence, enduring terrorist organizations (such as the IRA, the Liberation Tigers of Tamil Eelam (LTTE), the Kurdish Workers Party (PKK), and Hezbollah), with the organizational capacity to engage in larger-scale crime with higher profit margins, have turned to criminal activities to raise funds to support their activities.[10] Currently, drug trafficking is thought to be the most significant source of income for both terrorist and international criminal organizations.[11]

While the means of both organized-crime and terrorist groups have become more alike, their reputed ends remain conceptually distinct for most observers. In general, terrorism's primary goal is political and/or ideological, whereas organized crime is driven by financial motives. Terrorist organizations engage in criminal activity to advance their agendas—ideological, social, or political—whereas criminal organizations engage in violence to advance and/or protect their criminal agendas. Terrorist groups seek to destroy the status quo, while criminal syndicates seek stable shadow business environments.[12]

There seem to be distinguishing features in the criminality pursued by different terrorist groups, and "the opportunities and skills

---

[8] Canadian Centre for Intelligence and Security Studies, The Norman Patterson School of International Affairs, Carleton University, *Actual and Potential Links Between Terrorism and Criminality,* Volume 2006-5, Integrated Threat Assessment Centre, ITAC Trends in Terrorism Series, Vol. 5, No. 4, 2006, p. 5; Michael Buchanan, "London bombs cost just hundreds," *BBC News,* January 3, 2006.

[9] Joshua Prober, "Accounting for Terror: Debunking the Paradigm of Inexpensive Terrorism," *PolicyWatch/PeaceWatch,* Washington Institute for Near East Policy, PolicyWatch #1041. Available at http://www.washingtoninstitute.org/templateC05.php?CID=2389 (as of September 12, 2008).

[10] Canadian Centre for Intelligence and Security Studies, 2006, pp. 5–8.

[11] Ibid., p. 4.

[12] Chris Dishman, "Terrorism, Crime, and Transformation," *Studies in Conflict & Terrorism,* Vol. 24, No. 1, 2001.

associated with criminal successes and failures are contingent upon historical and cultural factors."[13] Radical Islamic terrorists require "low-level operatives to perform menial criminal acts . . . [and they] are recruited less for the criminal skills than for their connections to local communities." Conversely, "[domestic] right-wing groups recruit individuals specifically for their criminal skills." There are also useful patterns in criminal failure by terrorist organizations. The Islamic terrorists reportedly fail in several ways: Their crimes alienate the local communities upon which they depend; they face high barriers to international travel; they are inexperienced at concealing incriminating evidence; and they are usually unable to "transform opportunity into terrorism." Right-wing terrorists fail differently: They are poor at counterfeiting and maintaining internal security.

Logic suggests that organized-crime groups in general would hesitate to work with terrorist groups, either in selling goods and services to them or in using terrorist funding as capital in their illicit activities. The main reason is that organized crime fears that any association with terror groups will intensify the scrutiny of law enforcement, jeopardizing the criminals' operations and perhaps even their survival.[14] Criminals want to live to steal another day; they are not candidates for suicide bombing.

For their parts, terrorist groups have to fear that if they are too successful at crime, criminal groups will turn on them. Moreover, for cultural reasons, Islamic and other anti-Western terrorist groups might object to selling pirated American films, the symbols of the very society they wish to undo. Groups such as the Revolutionary Armed Forces of Colombia (FARC) and Mexico's Zapatista National Liberation Army (EZLN) have refused to engage in criminal activities that, even though

[13] All quotations in the paragraph are from Mark S. Hamm, *Crimes Committed by Terrorist Groups: Theory, Research, and Prevention*, Washington, D.C.: U.S. Department of Justice, Office of Justice Programs, June 1, 2005, pp. vii–viii. Available at http://www.ncjrs.gov/pdf-files1/nij/grants/211203.pdf (as of September 12, 2008).

[14] Jeanne K. Giraldo and Harold A. Trinkunas, "The Political Economy of Terrorist Financing," in Jeanne K. Giraldo and Harold A. Trinkunas (eds.), *Terrorism Financing and State Responses: A Comparative Perspective*, Stanford, CA: Stanford University Press, 2007, p. 19.

profitable, do not conform to the groups' pure ideological or political agenda.[15]

Overall, there is little evidence of clear and widespread ties between traditional organized-crime groups and terrorist organizations, yet connections do exist. Most known alliances are tacit, rather than explicit, and full convergence between the two types of groups is more likely for insurgent groups like the FARC or the IRA, which, in effect, aged from terror into pure criminality once the political issues were all but settled.[16] For their parts, major organized-crime groups such as the triads in Hong Kong or the Mafia in Sicily do not fit the classical definition of terrorist groups. Indeed, organized-crime groups rarely engage in terror—the Mexican drug traffickers' violence threatens the control of the Mexican state, but it is still selective violence, not pure terrorism.

Points of Convergence Between Terrorism and Organized Crime

There is, however, growing recognition that the intersection between organized crime and terror organizations is deepening and becoming more complex. New actors such as insurgents and gangs have joined the mix, and crime has become a critical source of funding for terrorist groups, including Hezbollah.[17] While this is happening in the United States, Italy, Canada, and other rich countries, it is perhaps happening even more in societies that are alienated from governments, where

---

[15] Dishman, 2001, p. 44.

[16] Tamara Makarenko identifies four major points of possible convergence between terror and criminal groups: alliances, operational motivations, convergence, and the "black hole" syndrome, in which the convergence between political and criminal motives of a single group allow it to dominate a state (see "A model of terrorist-criminal relations," *Jane's Intelligence Review*, August 2003, pp. 6–11).

[17] Michael P. Arena, "Hizballah's Global Criminal Operations," *Global Crime*, Vol. 7, No. 3–4, August–November 2006, p. 455.

the rule of law is not firmly entrenched, and where law enforcement is weak.[18] In many respects, that kind of environment is also one that fosters or permits terrorism. At the same time, alienation from government, a fuzzy rule of law, and weak enforcement are also factors that permit and sustain intellectual-property crimes.

A deeper look into history reveals that many fundamentalist terrorist groups have engaged in criminal enterprises that their religion would seem to proscribe. For example, in 1981, the terrorist group al-Jihad conducted a string of armed robberies against Christian-owned jewelry stores to finance the assassination of Egyptian President Anwar Sadat. To justify their action, they cited a passage in the Koran which affirms the right to "take spoils won in a war with infidels." Similarly, Hezbollah's original fatwa justified the financing of operations through selling drugs as a means of warfare against Americans and Jews: "If we cannot kill them with guns, so we will kill them with drugs."[19]

A special factor in the possible convergence of film piracy and terrorism might be the utility of film-pirating equipment (burners and camcorders) and film-piracy distribution networks for creating and disseminating propaganda. Terrorist groups produce high-quality multimedia materials to recruit supporters, train members, issue proclamations, and inspire fear in their enemies. Therefore, film-piracy operations could be dual-use, building profit but also enabling propaganda. Test purchases made near Peshawar in the North-West Frontier Province of Pakistan uncovered pirated American films with some ideological value intermixed among Jihadi propaganda. The film *Black Hawk Down*, which depicts the 1993 defeat of U.S. military forces in Somalia, was a popular item in stalls that distributed proclamations from Abu Musab al-Zarqawi, the leader of al Qaeda in Iraq (see Figure 2.1).

The intersection of crime and terrorism raises three important issues that have bearing on considerations of counterfeiting: First, to what extent do terrorist organizations have an "in-house" criminal capacity? In the words of one observer, "Some of the most serious ter-

---

[18] Canadian Centre for Intelligence and Security Studies, 2006, pp. 5–8.

[19] Phil Williams, *Organized Crime and Terrorism*, Washington, D.C.: Defense Intelligence Agency, Project on Terrorist Financing 2004–2005, 2005.

Figure 2.1
Test Purchase: Peshawar, Pakistan, November 2006

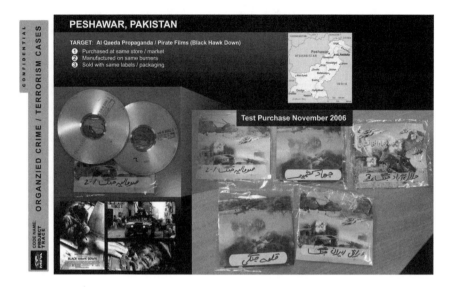

RAND *MG742-2.1*

rorism cases detected have not involved organized crime groups at all—the terrorists have acted alone using methods of organized crime."[20] Second, to what extent have criminal and terrorist organizations allied with each other in either parasitical or symbiotic ways? And third, to what extent have terrorists benefited indirectly from the proceeds of organized criminal activity, including piracy?

A list of terrorist organizations with reputed in-house and/or sizable criminal operations or capabilities might include Hezbollah, FARC, Egyptian Islamic Jihad, the Kosovo Liberation Army (KLA), the PKK, the Islamic Movement of Uzbekistan (IMU), the Provisional IRA, and the LTTE. These organizations engage in criminal enterprises across international borders, within their home countries, within

---

[20] Louise I. Shelley et al., *Methods and Motives: Exploring Links Between Transnational Organized Crime and International Terrorism*, Washington, D.C.: U.S. Department of Justice, Document Number 211207, June 23, 2005, p. 14. Available at http://www.ncjrs.gov/pdf-files1/nij/grants/211207.pdf (as of September 12, 2008).

diaspora communities (especially in North America), and in their areas of operation.[21]

There is also growing evidence of cooperation between terrorist organizations and organized crime, which again is most notable for the insurgent groups—Peru's Shining Path, FARC, M19 in Colombia, the LTTE, and the Palestinian Popular Front for the Liberation of Palestine–General Command (PFLP-GC) are reported to have provided security for narcotics cartels in their respective countries or regions.[22] In the Balkans and Central Asia, as well as Colombia, Myanmar, and Afghanistan, markets dominated by organized crime require terrorist organizations desiring entry to forge alliances.[23] "A process of 'gangsterization' may also occur where revolutionary and terrorist movements drift into money-making as a primary activity," with the Shan United Army of Burma, Shining Path, and the FARC cited as examples.[24] It could also be argued that Iraqi insurgents became similar as they began to resemble third-generation criminal gangs.[25]

Moreover, terrorists and criminals both operate "outside the law," and they often use the same methods, such as false identification and shipping documents and countersurveillance techniques.[26] Terrorists and pirates share other operational similarities: They are usually rational calculators, highly adaptive and resilient, and both equipped and inclined to use extortion, intimidation, and violence to control territories. Both types of organizations seem to be "flattening," as individual

---

[21] For a full list of terrorist organizations with criminal capabilities, see Makarenko, 2003, pp. 6–11.

[22] For a discussion of narco-terrorism links, see Sebastyen Gorka, "The 'New' Threat of Organised Crime and Terrorism," *Jane's Terrorism and Security Monitor*, June 1, 2000.

[23] Makarenko, 2003, pp. 6–11.

[24] This discussion of cooperation between organized-crime and terrorist organizations can be found, along with the quotation, in Canadian Centre for Intelligence and Security Studies, 2006, p. 10.

[25] Max G. Manwaring, *Street Gangs: The New Urban Insurgency*, Carlisle, PA: Strategic Studies Institute, U.S. Army War College, March 2005, pp. 8–12. Available at http://www.strategicstudiesinstitute.army.mil/pdffiles/PUB597.pdf (as of September 12, 2008).

[26] Thomas Sanderson, "Transnational Terror and Organized Crime: Blurring the Lines," *SAIS Review*, Vol. 24, No. 1, 2004.

actors operate more freely from the authority of a centralized head-quarters in order to escape official scrutiny.[27]

The distinction is further blurred by growing evidence that gangs are a prominent component in the crime-terrorism dynamic. For example, Dawood Ibrahim is India's godfather of godfathers who runs criminal gangs from Bangkok to Dubai. Ibrahim's gang syndicate, called D-Company, engages in strong-arm protection, drug trafficking, extortion, and murder-for-hire. He was implicated in the 1993 Mumbai bombings, and under Indian pressure, the U.S. Treasury Department designated Ibrahim a "global terrorist" for lending his smuggling infrastructure to al Qaeda, and supporting Islamic extremists in Pakistan.[28] D-Company activities associated with counterfeiting are detailed in Chapter Five.

Finally, terrorist groups may benefit indirectly from organized crime, including piracy, if crime groups, even groups motivated primarily by greed, are also sympathetic to movements that embrace terrorist wings. The detailed cases from the tri-border area of South America, presented in Chapter Six, are examples of this indirect benefit. These cases also illustrate the difficulties of unraveling the chain, since the money may flow first to either front groups or legitimate providers of social services and only later seep to terrorists or terror activities.

The Changing Face of Terrorism

The end of the Cold War both resulted from and removed many of the last barriers to globalization. It was thus a defining moment in the evolution of modern terrorism, most importantly in the area of terrorist finance.[29] The conventional reading of post-Cold War terrorism high-

---

[27] Chris Dishman, "The Leaderless Nexus: When Crime and Terror Converge," *Studies in Conflict & Terrorism*, Vol. 28, No. 3, 2005, p. 237.

[28] Gary I. Wilson and John P. Sullivan, *On Gangs, Crime, and Terrorism*, Special to Defense and the National Interest, February 28, 2007. Available at http://www.d-n-i.net/fcs/pdf/wilson_sullivan_gangs_terrorism.pdf (as of September 12, 2008).

[29] Giraldo and Trinkunas, 2007, p. 9.

lights two major changes, the decline of state and philanthropic forms of support. To those trends should be added a third, the globalization of organized crime.

The end of the superpower rivalry between the United States and the Soviet Union reduced the incentive for those countries to fund insurgents as proxies in ideological wars, and Soviet allies, if not Moscow itself, were linked to financing terrorists.[30] Less-polarized global politics induced prominent terrorist sponsors, such as Libya, to reconsider their policies.[31] Today, the number of "officially designated" sponsors has been reduced, and, indeed, only a few are really "active" (in particular, Iran). As a result, some of the governments that were suspected of being involved, directly or indirectly, in supporting terrorists (e.g., Saudi Arabia and Pakistan) are not on the U.S. list of state sponsors.[32] Furthermore, the (d)evolution to networked structures has eroded state control in some terrorist groups, and the move toward criminality has given terrorist organizations an independent cash flow they did not have before.[33]

Indeed, some terrorist groups have moved a considerable distance from playing a subordinate role in nation-state conflicts to becoming prominent as international influences in their own right. They are becoming more integrated with other non-state entities, such as criminal organizations and legitimately chartered corporations, and are gradually assuming various levels of control and identity with national governments. For example, the FARC and the National Liberation Army (ELN) of Colombia use extortion, kidnapping, money laundering, and other economic strategies to finance their operations. At the turn of the century, the FARC was already estimated to be collecting a half-billion dollars per year from protecting the drug trade in the

---

[30] Harvey Kushner, "The New Terrorism," in Harvey Kushner (ed.), *The Future of Terrorism: Violence at the New Millennium*, Thousand Oaks, CA: Sage, 1998, p. 4.

[31] Giraldo and Trinkunas, 2007, p. 9.

[32] The list currently includes Cuba, Iran, North Korea, Sudan, and Syria. Available at http://www.state.gov/s/ct/rls/crt/2007/103711.htm (as of September 23, 2008).

[33] This theme runs through the chapters in Giraldo and Trinkunas, 2007.

region.[34] Other examples include Hezbollah and HAMAS members who establish front companies to cover an illegal market system and to conduct money laundering, fraud, and tax evasion. U.S. investigations have directly named Hezbollah and HAMAS as recipients of profits from illegal cigarette smuggling, profits that also provide material support to terrorism.[35]

This evolution has inverted the previous relationship between terrorists and governments. In the old pattern, state sponsors had a measure of control over "their" terrorist groups. Now, because terrorist groups can generate income from both legitimate and illegal sources, the terrorist organization often "sponsors" and props up its weaker partner, a national government.[36] For example, while Taliban-controlled Afghanistan was crucial in al Qaeda's development, the terrorist organization was hardly hostage to its host. During the period when it was based in Afghanistan, al Qaeda was running an annual operating budget of approximately $200 million, compared with its host's budget of $70 million.[37] Older groups, such as the Palestine Liberation Organization (PLO), attained some autonomy by leveraging donations, extortions, and extralegal sources into investments. In the 1980s, the PLO was estimated to be receiving as much as four-fifths of its annual operating budget of $600 million from investments.[38]

The September 11, 2001, attacks were testimony to the fact that global arrangements to counter terrorism had not developed quickly

---

[34] Christopher C. Harmon, *Terrorism Today*, London and Portland, OR: Frank Cass, 2000, pp. 65 and 139.

[35] William Billingslea, "Illicit Cigarette Trafficking and the Funding of Terrorism," *The Police Chief*, February 2004, pp. 49–54.

[36] Maurice R. Greenberg et al., *Terrorist Financing: Report of an Independent Task Force Sponsored by the Council on Foreign Relations*, New York: Council on Foreign Relations, November 25, 2002, p. 5.

[37] David Albright, *Al Qaeda's Nuclear Program: Through the Window of Seized Documents*, Policy Forum Online Special Forum 47, November 6, 2002, p. 8. Available at http://www.nautilus.org/fora/Special-Policy-Forum/47_Albright.html (as of September 12, 2008).

[38] Bruce Hoffman, *Inside Terrorism*, New York: Columbia University Press, 1998, p. 84.

enough, but they surely did provide an incentive to do better.[39] It is important not to overstate the amount of improvement that has been achieved, but in the area of counterterrorist finance, new norms and best practices have been broadly accepted in the financial community, helping to stanch the flow of philanthropic funding of terrorism.[40] This loss has reinforced the loss of state sponsorship in pushing terrorist groups toward crime. Nor is crime really new as a source of funding—Marxist-Leninist terrorist groups of the 1960s and 1970s relied on kidnapping and robbery to supplement state sponsorship. And, as the case study on Northern Ireland indicates, the IRA had turned to crime before the end of the Cold War, when the U.S. government cracked down on private sources of funding in the U.S. Irish diaspora.[41]

What the drying-up of state sponsorship and private funding required, globalization facilitated—unprecedented opportunities for criminal activity, along with more-diverse interactions between terrorists and criminals and a "wider range of illicit financing sources" than often is assumed.[42] In the long list of crimes used by terrorists for financing, many are characterized by lower barriers to entry in an era of globalization—for instance, smuggling commodities (from precious metals to cigarettes), smuggling people, kidnapping, credit-card theft, and trafficking.[43]

In summary, the usual distinction between terrorist and criminal organizations is really a continuum, with purely financial motives at one extreme and purely ideological or political objectives at the other. The debate about their precise purposes will continue, but most terrorist groups have had to move toward the middle of the continuum, embracing both criminal activities and attendant violence to sustain their ultimate objectives. For practical purposes, terrorist and organized-

---

[39] Anne L. Cunan, "U.S. and International Responses," in Giraldo and Trinkunas, 2007, p. 274.

[40] Ibid., p. 260.

[41] Giraldo and Trinkunas, 2007, p. 10.

[42] John T. Picarelli and Louise Shelly, "The Political Economy of Terrorist Financing," in Giraldo and Trinkunas, 2007, p. 40.

[43] Ibid., p. 47.

crime organizations may, at certain junctures, find it useful to cooperate with each other in furtherance of their respective goals. Why each group is doing this is not necessarily as immediately compelling as the fact that they are doing so, and it is imperative that policymakers and law enforcement organizations understand this process in order to exploit vulnerabilities in both forms of organization.

In response to the September 11 attacks, the United States and other nations rapidly shifted efforts from transnational crime to the threat of terrorism. Between 2000 and 2003, FBI organized-crime and narcotics units lost 758 agents to counterterrorism.[44] Now, however, as terrorism becomes more homegrown and cells spring up that may be inspired by but are not much directed from abroad, countering it has more and more in common with operations against drug traffickers or organized crime. The intelligence task puts a premium on unraveling networks that can span countries and continents. As a result, police departments need to reengage their organized-crime units in the fight against terrorism.[45] They need to be especially on the lookout for criminal enterprises that might serve as the infrastructure for terrorism, including its funding. And counterfeiting is attractive because it is profitable and not hard to enter.[46]

---

[44] Moises Naim, quoting a 2004 report issued by the Inspector General of the Department of Justice, in *Illicit: How Smugglers, Traffickers and Copycats Are Hijacking the Global Economy*, London: William Heinemann, 2006, p. 179.

[45] Robert Dreyfuss, "The Cops Are Watching You," *The Nation*, June 3, 2002.

[46] Lieutenant John C. Stedman, County of Los Angeles Sheriff's Department, CQ Congressional Testimony, Capitol Hill Hearing Testimony, Committee on Senate Homeland Security and Governmental Affairs, May 25, 2005.

CHAPTER THREE

The Shape of Counterfeiting and the Example of Film Piracy

Why might organized crime or terrorist groups be attracted to counterfeiting? The easy answer is profit, and lots of it at minimum risk compared with many more-capital-intensive and higher-risk illicit activities that they already engage in, such as drug and human trafficking. Consider this: A blank optical disc costs as little as 20 cents in the United States (and is free if it is stolen), while counterfeits can sell for many times that amount, from 35 baht (about $1 at 2008 exchange rates) from vendors in Bangkok, to $5 in the streets of New York's Chinatown, or as much as $18 if the counterfeit is passed off as a legal copy.

Factors Fueling Counterfeiting

The financial and technical barriers to entry in counterfeiting many products are low. Film piracy is an especially striking example because the barriers are probably lower for it than for counterfeiting other products. Virtually anyone can start an optical-disc counterfeiting operation. Someone with several hundred dollars can begin a mini-piracy operation with a few hundred blank optical discs, DVD burners that cost less than $100 each from a local computer store, and legal movie discs that cost less than $20 each from a retail store, although many pirated movies can also be obtained at no cost over the Internet. A few thousand dollars can establish a fairly sizable operation capable of producing hundreds, if not thousands, of counterfeit film discs every day.[1]

Such an operation, with or without the involvement of organized crime, can be set up in a single room or apartment and be up and running within a matter of hours. Also, turnover is quick, and counterfeit DVDs are a cash-and-carry item. Within 24 hours of setting up a counterfeit operation, fake DVDs could hit the streets and be sold for cash at the street prices described above to bring in handsome profits. Indeed, the profit margins (though not yet the total profits) are very high, much higher than those for drugs, for instance. In one recent estimate, the cost of copying a computer program is about 30 cents, while the counterfeit program might sell for more than $50. In contrast, a gram of marijuana was estimated to cost around $2.25 to produce and would sell for about $18.[2] A second estimate, issued in 2005 by the UK National Criminal Intelligence Service (NCIS), found that a DVD manufactured in Malaysia for about $0.70 was marked up more than 1,150 percent and sold on the streets of London for the equivalent of $9. The cross-border markup is three times higher than the markup for Iranian heroin and higher than that for Colombian cocaine.[3]

Moreover, even if counterfeiters get caught, the penalties are relatively slight. In 2003, Interpol Secretary General Ronald Noble acknowledged in testimony before the U.S. Congress that one of the greatest attractions of DVD piracy continued to be its relatively low risk compared with other criminal activity. In the European destination markets, statutes are for the most part also more lenient for copyright

---

[1] According to Felton's "routine activity theory," in the absence of effective controls, offenders will prey on attractive targets if they are at the same place—an object for property crimes, a person for personal crimes. If the controllers are absent, or present but powerlessness, crime is possible. See Marcus Felson, *Crime and Everyday Life: Insight and Implications for Society,* Thousand Oaks, CA: Pine Forge Press, 1994.

[2] Union de Fabricants, *Counterfeiting and Organized Crime,* 2003, p. 10. Available at http://www.interpol.int/public/financialcrime/intellectualproperty/publications/udfcounterfeiting.pdf (as of September 13, 2008).

[3] UK National Criminal Intelligence Service SU/Drug Project, 2004. Cocaine markup is from Colombia to Spain/UK; heroin markup is from Iran to UK; DVD markup is from Malaysia to UK.

offenses. For instance, under French law, selling counterfeit products is punishable by a two-year prison term and a 150,000 fine, while selling drugs is punishable by a ten-year prison term and a 7,500,000 fine. In the United States, more than a million and a half people were arrested for drug-related offenses in 2003.[4] The previous year, the most recent year for which the U.S. Department of Justice provides updated data, 134 defendants were sentenced for intellectual-property infringement-related offenses in U.S. federal courts.[5] In California, the sentence for a first offense of an intellectual property rights (IPR) crime—which includes most counterfeiting—is usually probation. Moreover, "three strikes" laws mandating minimum sentences after a third offense do not apply, since IPR crimes are not violent.[6]

Small wonder, then, that one suspect referring to disc piracy said to the Los Angeles Sheriff's Department: "It's better than the dope business, no one's going to prison for DVDs."[7] The dilemma here, though, is that merely raising the penalties for convicted street peddlers is not enough; indeed, some of them may be victims themselves, forced to sell pirated goods to pay off debts to the smugglers who brought them into the country illegally or loaned them money at usurious rates. Therefore, a more effective deterrent strategy would have to be based on the readiness to pursue the connections between street peddling and organized crime.

The piracy of movies, software, games, and other digital products is occurring against a larger backdrop of technology change. Blank discs and DVD burners are not expensive. DVD players, too, are getting cheaper by the day. Widespread access to computers, the Internet,

---

[4] U.S. Department of Justice, Office of Justice Programs, Bureau of Justice Statistics, *Drug and Crime Facts, Arrest Seizures,* 2003. Available at http://www.ojp.usdoj.gov/bjs/dcf/enforce.htm (as of August 1, 2008).

[5] Mark Motivans, *Intellectual Property Theft,* 2002, U.S. Department of Justice, Bureau of Justice Statistics, October 2004. Available at http://www.ojp.usdoj.gov/bjs/pub/pdf/ipt02.pdf (as of September 13, 2008).

[6] William F. Bratton, "The Mutation of the Illegal Trade Market," *The Police Chief,* May 2007, p. 23.

[7] Stedman, 2005.

and broadband access, as well as computing know-how in developed as well as developing societies, means there are more people able to and with the means to download movies—legally or illegally—and sell them to counterfeiting operations or reproduce them for sale.

Nor does the sale of counterfeit DVDs require any specialized sales infrastructure or support. The advertising is done by the major movie studios. All the pirates need do is counterfeit discs and cover jackets with titles and pictures of actors printed on them. They can get counterfeit artwork for DVD titles that are still in theaters on websites for free. Hence, as our case studies also show, it is not surprising that Asian organized-crime groups in Britain can compel persons they smuggled in from China, for example, to sell counterfeit DVDs in pubs and on the street to pay off their debts; indeed, the groups compel the illegal immigrants to work in all facets of the piracy operation, from reproduction to distribution. To be able to sell, all they need is the ability to say "three pounds"—the typical street price for a counterfeit disc in Britain—or display three fingers if they cannot manage the words.

Consuming DVDs is even easier, and it is less risky than consuming other kinds of counterfeit goods. Consumers need not worry about any adverse impact on their health or the safety of their home from the use of counterfeit DVDs. Unlike fake medicines that might sicken (or even kill) them or electrical appliances that might short-circuit and start fires, the worst that can happen is that a counterfeit optical disc is such a poor copy that the movie cannot be watched. Further, people who buy counterfeit DVDs for their personal consumption are rarely, if ever, arrested by law enforcement. While the purchase of a pirated DVD is illegal in some countries, such as Italy, confiscation of the property, a verbal reprimand, or, in even rarer cases, a small fine is usually the most severe penalty that will be applied.

The low barrier to entry and the promise of high profits at low risk are major reasons why film piracy is rampant across virtually the entire world, and particularly the developing world. The other reason is demand. The enormous demand for pirated films is, in some cases, intensified by government policies. For example, the Chinese government allows a maximum of only 20 foreign films per year into China for theater viewing.[8] As more and more Chinese have both money and access to what is hot in the global village, that policy virtually ensures that they will turn to counterfeit DVDs to access foreign films. Just as the prohibition of alcohol spurred its illegal production and fueled the growth of organized-crime groups in the United States in the 1920s and early 1930s, China's policy spurs optical-disc piracy and counterfeiting to satisfy a market demand. The fact that optical-disc players sell for as little as $35 to $40 in China means that over 100 million households in a country of 1 billion people are ready consumers of counterfeit pirated films.[9] In other countries, such as South Korea, where computer penetration is high, consumers view pirated films on their computers or other portable electronic devices.

To be sure, demand for counterfeit films exists even when legal means to obtain films on DVD are available. The low prices of pirated films compared with legal ones make the former very attractive to buyers. Movies often are "consumed" only once, which means there is less incentive to pay more for a high-quality product: Why pay more for a legal copy when a counterfeit suffices? Many consumers do not want to wait for legal copies that might take months, if not longer, to show up in stores. They also do not want to wait when they know their peers in other parts of the world are already seeing the films. The Internet, satellite television, radio, and other media provide rapid access to information to consumers everywhere about what is happening elsewhere in the world.

For young people, in particular, the real and marketed sense of a global community and culture also provide motivation to want access to films and other commodities as soon as their peers have it. Recognizing that, movie studies often release major films, such as *Spiderman 3*, in many cities across the globe at the same time. If a blockbuster is

---

[8] Patrick Frater, "Hollywood weighs ying and yang of China," *Variety*, August 4, 2008. Available at http://www.varietyasiaonline.com/content/view/6622/53/ (as of September 13, 2008).

[9] Patrick Frater, "China DVD Market Poised for Fourfold Growth," *Variety*, March 6, 2007. Fraser estimates that there will be DVD players in 143 million Chinese households by 2010. Available at http://www.varietyasiaonline.com/content/view/899/53 (as of September 13, 2008).

released on the big screen on a Friday in New York, young people from Nairobi to Rio, from Shanghai to Mumbai, will want to enjoy the experience at the same time, not months later, and will want to have the convenience of enjoying it at home.

Demand for such illegal goods is also spurred by the global migration of people and their desire for access to news, entertainment, and other media products from their home countries or cultural and linguistic heritage. While Hollywood movies are the most visible targets of pirates, movies and television programs produced locally in India, Hong Kong, Nigeria, Thailand, and elsewhere are also targets. In contrast to Hollywood films, which may have broad appeal to consumers across cultural and linguistic groups, pirated movies and television programs from other places are typically consumed only by particular cultural and linguistic groups that find them of interest.

Pirated films are more likely to be found in retail outlets that cater to such cultural and linguistic groups—for instance, counterfeit Hong Kong movies at Chinese grocery stores or Hindi movies at Indian groceries and video rental stores around the world. Pirated copies are easily available even when legitimate ones are also available. In the past, when local networks, cable, and satellite television did not offer films from Hong Kong and India, buying or renting counterfeit copies was the only option for access. In Pakistan, for instance, the distribution of Indian films was illegal for more than 40 years until the ban was lifted in 2006 as a gesture of goodwill in peace talks. Thus, until 2006, the only way for Pakistanis to see Indian movies was to buy counterfeit copies smuggled into the country.[10] Today, as international distribution of local film titles has matured, well-entrenched demand for and supply of pirated films hit these local film industries especially hard, since they are much less able to sustain the losses than the major Hollywood studios are.[11]

---

[10] "Pakistan to Show Bollywood Film," *BBC News*, January 23, 2006. Available at http://news.bbc.co.uk/2/hi/entertainment/4639216.stm (as of September 13, 2008); Randeep Ramesh, "Bollywood love story: Pakistan lifts ban on Indian films," *The Guardian*, January 23, 2006, p. 19.

[11] However, in the absence of any legal market, Indian filmmakers might have condoned—even supported—smuggling, hoping to attract future customers, if not current ones (much as cigarette companies have done).

The Color of Money

If the barriers to entry in counterfeiting, along with the risks, are low, the financial rewards are high. The Organisation for Economic Co-operation and Development (OECD) estimates that at least $200 billion of international trade in 2005 was in counterfeited products,[12] and that did not include pirated products made and consumed within a single country or counterfeit products distributed over the Internet. The losses to the industry are not the same as the profits to the pirates—indeed, pirate profits could even be greater than industry losses because a thief's profit margins are far greater.

Plainly, estimating losses accurately is difficult. In the case of film piracy, for example, not everyone who bought a pirated DVD would have acquired a legitimate copy, much less paid for a premium seat in a theater. A 2005 study undertaken by the MPA attempted to account for this by factoring into the model a "substitution rate," that is, a rate from a global survey of a statistically significant number of moviegoers (those who had seen a movie in the previous month) in 22 countries. The estimates rely on those being interviewed to be both honest and self-aware about what their legitimate viewing consumption would have been had pirated alternatives not been available. For the purposes of this report, we had no need to dig deeply into how the estimates were reached, but the methods clearly address the challenges, combining macroeconomic data with survey accounts of the behavior of the pirates.

With all these caveats, according to a study that was undertaken by the MPA, film piracy cost the global industry more than $18 billion in 2005 (out of a total industry of $400 billion), of which about three-fifths was attributable to DVD piracy and two-fifths to online

---

[12] Organisation for Economic Co-operation and Development, *The Economic Impact of Counterfeiting and Piracy: Part IV. Executive Summary*, Directorate for Science, Technology and Industry, Committee on Industry, Innovation and Entrepreneurship, JT03228347, DSTI/IND(2007)9/PART4/REV1, June 4, 2007, p. 2. Available at http://www.oecd.org/dataoecd/11/38/38704571.pdf (as of September 13, 2008).

piracy.[13] Revenue loss to the member companies of the MPA was more than $6 billion. According to one economist, these losses to the major Hollywood studios in 2005, while substantial in and of themselves, do not reflect the true costs to the U.S. economy from film piracy. By this economist's estimate, the total cost to the U.S. economy was 141,030 jobs that would otherwise have been created (46,597 in the motion picture industry and 94,433 in ancillary industries); $5.5 billion in lost earnings; $837 million in lost tax revenues at the federal, state, and local levels; and $20.5 billion in total lost output among all U.S. industries.[14]

Most of the production, distribution, and consumption of pirated materials occurs in countries other than the United States. In much of the developing world, the piracy industry is so pervasive that it is all but impossible to buy legitimate film DVDs. And the efficiency of operations on this underside of globalization rivals that on the legitimate side. Pirated copies of movies usually appear both online and in DVD form within days and sometimes hours after the films' first worldwide theatrical release. The countries where film piracy is most active, according to one source, include Bolivia, Brazil, China, Colombia, Indonesia, Kazakhstan, Kuwait, Lithuania, Malaysia, Pakistan, Romania, Russia, and Ukraine.[15] While consumption of counterfeit products varies by region—the Middle East, for example, consumes the highest level of counterfeit automotive parts—consumption of pirated music, movies, and software "appears to be significant in all economies."[16]

---

[13] *Motion Picture Association Piracy Loss Estimate Study, 2005*, cited in Dan Glickman, "Film Piracy," interview, *C-Span*, 201096-1, Washington, D.C. Available at http://www.cspanarchives.org/library/index.php?main_page=product_video_info&products_id=201096-1 (as of September 13, 2008).

[14] Stephen E. Siwek, *The True Cost of Motion Picture Piracy to the U.S. Economy*, Institute for Policy Innovation, IPI Center for Technology Freedom, Policy Report 186, 2006, pp. 1–31. Available at http://www.nbcuni.com/About_NBC_Universal/Intellectual_Property/pdf/Motion_Picture_Piracy.pdf (as of September 13, 2008).

[15] Majid Yar, "The Global 'Epidemic' of Movie 'Piracy': Crime-Wave or Social Construction?" *Media, Culture & Society*, Vol. 27, No. 5, 2005, p. 680.

[16] Organisation for Economic Co-operation and Development, 2007.

In any case, criminal proceeds are fungible, and profits from counterfeiting can fund startups in other criminal enterprises, or vice versa. It is all money. In 2003, Thai authorities discovered and stopped a criminal trade in which proceeds from marijuana sales were reinvested in acquiring counterfeit goods intended for sale in France. A case involving financing in the opposite direction occurred in Mexico in 2002, where proceeds derived from the sale of counterfeit CDs were most likely reinvested in drug trafficking and in running a prostitution ring.[17]

The individuals profiled in this report's cases are not "rebels" who pirate movies because they see their action as standing up to multibillion-dollar corporations. Nor are they people who copy legally purchased or rented DVDs for personal use or for free distribution. Members of organized-crime groups conduct these acts of film piracy for financial gain and frequently engage in a range of other more destructive criminal activities. This chapter closes by examining film piracy as an example of counterfeiting, capturing the role of organized crime as an introduction to the detailed cases in the following chapters.

Defining Film Piracy

Film piracy constitutes an intellectual-property crime (IPC), which "refers to counterfeited and pirated goods, manufactured and sold for profit without the consent of the patent or trademark holder."[18] It

---

[17] Union de Fabricants, *Counterfeiting and Organised Crime Report,* 3rd ed., Paris, 2005, p. 19. Available at http://www.unifab.com/publications/cf_organised_crime_2edition.pdf (as of September 13, 2008).

[18] Northern Ireland Organized Crime Task Force, *The Threat Assessment 2002: Serious and Organised Crime in Northern Ireland.* Available at http://www.nio.gov.uk/organised_crime_ threat_assessment_2002.pdf (as of September 13, 2008). Intellectual property "refers to the legal rights that correspond to intellectual activity in the industrial, scientific, and artistic fields. These legal rights, most commonly in the form of patents, trademarks, and copyright, protect the moral and economic rights of the creators, in addition to the creativity and dissemination of their work. Industrial property, which is part of intellectual property, extends protection to inventions and industrial designs" (Ronald K. Noble, "The Links Between Intellectual Property Crime and Terrorist Financing," Testimony before the United States

comes in a number of forms, depending on how the original film is obtained and how the illegal copies are reproduced and distributed. The size of the economic blow dealt to a copyright owner, and thus the economic gain available to a pirate, is directly proportional to the time at which an original is stolen. A disproportionate amount of revenue— sometimes as much as one-quarter of the total made on a film in theatrical, DVD, and television form—is made in the first two weeks the film is in theaters. Not surprisingly, then, the reward to a pirate for stealing the first copy is significant, perhaps several hundred dollars for the first master, often with the possibility of selling multiple copies of that master to different pirate groups and of additional profits from the manufacture and distribution of pirate DVDs from that master.

The initial theft and the subsequent reproduction and distribution are two different activities with different types of actors and important implications for understanding the involvement of organized crime. Figure 3.1 summarizes the range of activities in film piracy.

On the reproduction and distribution side, film piracy divides between DVDs (or VCDs, which are popular in Asia, or VHS tapes, which are still popular in some countries) and downloads, but, as Figure 3.1 suggests, any of the ways of stealing a film can then feed into distribution through either DVDs or downloads, or both.

As the table shows, there are a number of ways that originals are stolen, including (1) by camcording in a theater[19]; (2) by leaking or stealing the print of a film in or en route to the theater—the vast majority of films are still distributed to movie houses physically, not digitally; (3) through a post-production leak—once "finished" by the studio, films go to post-production facilities for color enhancement and the like; (4) through a leak from a hospitality window (airline or hotel in-room pay-per-view)—again, films are sent to separate facilities to be turned into cartridges or other forms suitable for airlines and hotels;

House Committee on International Relations, 108th Cong., July 16, 2003, p. 2. Available at http://www.interpol.int/Public/ICPO/speeches/SG20030716.asp?HM=1 (as of September 13, 2008)).

[19] The industry estimates, on the basis of sophisticated forensic analysis of pirated films, that approximately 90 percent of initial appearances of new pirated films result from illegal camcording.

Figure 3.1
Stages and Forms of Film Piracy

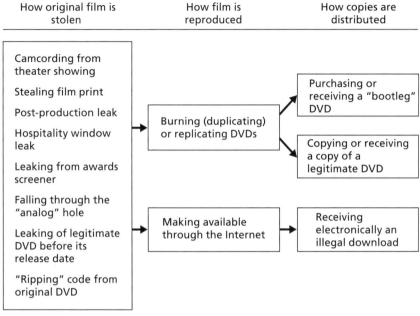

How original film is stolen	How film is reproduced	How copies are distributed

RAND *MG742-3.1*

(5) through a leak or theft from an awards screener, such as a screener for the Academy Awards; (6) by obtaining a film that is converted from digital (pay-per-view/cable) to analog and thus stripped of encryption; (7) by leaking or stealing a legitimately produced DVD prior to its official release date; or (8) by "ripping" a legitimately distributed DVD of any protective code—there are several free software and inexpensive hardware tools that can be used to accomplish this.

However the original is stolen, it can then be passed to pirates who "burn" (using a burning tower) or replicate (using a large commercial-grade replication machine) copies for sale by street vendors, or upload for distribution online, or, more often, do both simultaneously. Online groups (called warez, pronounced "wears," groups, also called encoding groups or release groups) began as a culture quite distinct from DVD pirates. They obtain a film (usually an illegal camcording); prepare it for online distribution, usually by compressing and digitizing the file; and then post it on a privately controlled, high-powered server called a top site, where it is made available to that group's members and everyone else who has access to the site.

Initially, these warez groups were driven by the challenge rather than by money; indeed, evidence of financial interest elicited scorn from fellow warez members. Now, however, while many upper-echelon members of warez groups are driven by the challenge, by wanting access to free goods, and by the thrill of "living on the edge," not to mention "street cred[it]" among the groups, there are some who make money. Moreover, there are many more people further downstream who are motivated by money and who make a lot of it by reproducing and distributing pirated films online. Warez groups are clearly organized and engaged in what is criminal activity—illegally profiting from stolen goods. As far as can be determined, however, they do not engage in other forms of organized crime, such as drug or human trafficking. This report addresses only the first row of the second column in Figure 3.1, the burning or otherwise copying of illegal DVDs for subsequent distribution and sale. This is where the money is to be made—for organized crime and for terrorists as well.

CHAPTER FOUR

Getting Down to Cases: Organized Crime and Film Piracy

The following cases, many of which are very well documented in court papers, offer a rare glimpse inside the operations of organized-crime groups profiting from film piracy. For ease of reading, this chapter and Chapters Five and Six present summaries of the case studies and citations to only some of the available documentation. Each of the case studies is described in greater detail and with fuller documentation in the Appendixes. Examining the array of case studies in full drives home the point that the three main features of piracy—low barrier to entry, high profit, and low risk—have made it a lucrative line of business for organized crime, alongside other criminal enterprises (see Table 4.1).

Organized crime's involvement in counterfeiting may be better understood by considering three motivations: consolidating, expanding vertically, and expanding horizontally. In the first, as the enry barrier to piracy is lowered, organized crime entrenches itself in the activity in order to fend off amateur competitors. In the second, a criminal group expands into piracy to derive profit from experience in related criminal activity. For instance, the methods used in human smuggling—forging documents, laundering money, smuggling objects or people across borders, and the like—can be leveraged when turning to piracy and vice-versa. The third, and most prevalent, motivation is expanding into piracy to diversify a criminal group's illicit revenue streams.

The three motivations are hardly mutually exclusive. They may be more useful for understanding than for guiding anti-piracy policy or operations. Yet they do provide some hints to what law enforcement

Table 4.1
Overview of Case Studies of Organized Crime and Piracy

Organized-Crime Group	Base Location	Film Piracy	Counterfeiting	Racketeering	Human Smuggling	Money Laundering/ Illegal Money Transfer Service	Illegal Gambling	Loan-Sharking	Narcotics Trafficking	Prostitution	Weapon Trafficking	Contract Killing	Document Forgery Services
Big Circle Boys	Canada	×	×	×	×	×	×	×	×	×	×	×	×
Yi Ging	USA	×		×		×	×	×	×				
Jah organization	USA	×				×							×
Cockle-picker gangmaster	England	×	×		×								
Lotus Trading Company	England	×	×		×								
Madrid Human smuggling ring	Spain	×			×								
Camorra Mafia	Italy	×	×	×	×	×	×	×	×	×	×	×	×
Wo Shing Wo triad	Hong Kong	×	×	×	×	×	×	×	×	×	×	×	×
San Yee On triad	Hong Kong	×	×	×	×	×	×	×	×	×	×	×	×
Ang Bin Hoey triad	Malaysia	×	×	×	×	×	×	×	×	×	×	×	×

might look for—for instance, the logic of vertical expansion makes piracy and human smuggling a more likely set of paired crimes than they might initially seem to be.

North America

The United States is a major market for pirated films, and police and other sources suggest that ethnic Asian gangs are involved in all aspects of optical-disc piracy, from stealing original material to reproduction, importing, and sales.[1] Most of the pirated discs that are sold in the United States come from U.S. burning labs, although some are ordered from DVD websites, many of which are based outside the United States, and pirated discs of some Chinese and Indian films are imported into ethnic communities in the United States.

Although some illegal camcordings are used exclusively by local pirate syndicates to supply local markets, most camcordings, many of which still are created in the United States and Canada, are provided to release groups or DVD pirate syndicates in China, Malaysia, Mexico, Russia, and elsewhere. For example, while there are large burning operations in Canada that supply big malls (such as Pacific Mall in Toronto), as well as Canadian groups that sell large amounts of pirated DVDs made from high-quality illegal camcordings from Canadian theaters over the Internet (such as Sportsmaniac.com and other affiliated sites which were raided and shut down by the Royal Canadian Mounted Police (RCMP) in December 2007), most of the downloads and pirated discs containing copies of those camcordings are produced and distributed overseas, not in Canada.

The Canadian government's Criminal Intelligence Service reports that Asian-based organized-crime groups in the lower mainland of

---

[1] Etan Vlessing, "Canada piracy provokes Fox threat," January 24, 2007, available at www.hollywoodreporter.com (as of October 1, 2008); Jim Kouri, "Major Chinese crime gang dismantled in New York," *American Chronicle*, September 12, 2005; Will Knight, "Insiders blamed for most online movie piracy," *New Scientist*, September 20, 2003, available at www.newscientist.com (as of October 1, 2008); RAND interviews with Hong Kong Customs Police, November 2007.

British Columbia are involved in large-scale importing and distribution of counterfeit tobacco and consumer goods, in particular, movies and music recordings.[2] Many are also involved in cybercrimes such as identity theft and are engaged in the reproduction of fraudulent credit cards, phone cards, and hotel card keys.[3] For example, the Big Circle Boys, born of the Red Guards and specializing in loan-sharking and drugs, are among many Asian organized-crime groups dealing in counterfeit goods, including pirated films.[4]

A July 2003 report found that in 2000, the Big Circle Boys had cells throughout North America.[5] The report emphasized their willingness to cooperate with ethnically diverse groups and their extensive involvement in the Southeast Asian heroin trade and credit-card counterfeiting.[6] A criminal organization called the 14K triad is the fastest-growing such group in Canada and has a presence in New York and other U.S. cities, as well.[7] Vietnamese gangs are also expanding rapidly into high-tech crimes.[8] DVDs manufactured in Asia have been found shipped to North America for sale.[9] The booming trade between Asia, and Canada and the United States, and the growth of a large Asian immigration community have apparently enabled Sun Yee On, one

---

[2] Neil S. Helfand, *Asian Organized Crime and Terrorist Activity in Canada, 1999–2002*, Washington, D.C.: Library of Congress, Federal Research Division, July 2003. Available at http://www.loc.gov/rr/frd/pdf-files/AsianOrgCrime_Canada.pdf (as of September 9, 2008).

[3] Ibid.

[4] Neal Hall, "Big Circle Boys born of Red Guards: Drugs, loansharking among Asian gang specialties," *Vancouver Sun*, June 10, 2005; Jennifer Bolz, "Chinese Organized Crime and Illegal Alien Trafficking: Humans as a Commodity," and "Trademark Counterfeiting," Hearing before the Committee on the Judiciary United States Senate, 104th Cong., 1st sess. on S.1136, a bill to control and prevent commercial counterfeiting, and for other purposes, October 10, 1995, Serial no. J-104-49.

[5] Helfand, 2003.

[6] Ibid.

[7] James O. Finckenauer and Ko-lin Chin, *Asian Transnational Organized Crime*, U.S. Department of Justice, Office of Justice Programs, National Institute of Justice Special Report, January 2007.

[8] Ibid.

[9] Ibid.

of the most powerful Chinese triad groups with deep roots in Hong Kong, to operate in a number of Canadian cities.[10]

The Yi Ging: Chinatown Gang in New York City[11]

From 2000 to 2005, the Yi Ging organization was a menacing presence in Manhattan's Chinatown and the Flushing neighborhood of Queens.[12] Its criminal enterprises ranged from DVD and CD piracy to extortion, gambling, witness tampering, and narcotics distribution.

- **Highlight.** This case was one of the first in which the Racketeer Influenced and Corrupt Organizations (RICO) Act was used to prosecute the participants in a conspiracy that included film piracy along with other criminal activities.
- **Piracy revenues.** Federal authorities believe that the Yi Ging's piracy business alone netted some $1.2 million a year. Overall, the indictment seeks a total $10 million in asset forfeiture. The gang went to great lengths to protect this revenue stream, using tactics including threats of violence and the destruction of a rival group's DVD-R facility.
- **Discovery of piracy.** The Yi Ging's piracy activity first came to the attention of authorities in 2000 in a raid of a piracy retail front located at 24 East Broadway, New York City. The indictment states that the gang's activity in later years included the operation of at least two gambling dens, loan-sharking, extortion, and trafficking of the narcotics ketamine and Ecstasy.
- **Motivation for entry into piracy.** The Yi Ging case study exhibits both consolidation and horizontal-expansion connections between organized crime and piracy. Piracy enabled the organi-

---

[10] Don Liddick and Ronald R. Liddick, *The Global Underworld: Transnational Crime and the United States*, Westport, CT: Greenwood Publishing Group, 2004; International Crime Threat Assessment, available at http://clinton4.nara.gov/WH/EOP/NSC/html/documents/pub45270/pub45270index.html (as of October 1, 2008).

[11] See Appendix A, pp. 1–5, for a more detailed description of this case.

[12] United States District Court for the Southern District of New York (Foley Square), Yi Ging Indictment Count 1, Sec 2, p. 4.

zation to consolidate control over its territory and also provided proceeds to support other criminal activities.

- **Role of law enforcement.** The multidefendant, multicount indictment followed simultaneous investigations by the FBI, the New York Police Department (NYPD), and the federal Bureau of Immigration and Customs Enforcement (ICE), working alongside industry over the course of five years.
- **Evidence base.** The indictment provides an exceptionally well-documented look into the gang's criminal activity, the brutality it used to enforce rackets, and the money-laundering techniques it used to hide the proceeds of its piracy enterprises.

In September 2005, a federal grand jury in New York returned a multicount indictment against several members of the Yi Ging organization, including several charges alleging violations of the federal RICO Act (P.L. 91-452 §901[a]), the first application of RICO to intellectual-property theft. The massive indictment covered a broad range of organized criminal activity and illicit businesses, including a multi-million-dollar piracy business based on the sale of illegal DVDs manufactured in China. The gang members were charged with 21 other offenses in addition to racketeering—the most notable of which were assault, extortion, conspiracy, extortionate debt collection, witness tampering, money laundering, gambling, drug trafficking, and trafficking in counterfeit DVDs and CDs.

The leadership of the organization consisted of Geng Chen (leader) and Kai Zhi Wang (deputy).[13] Film and music piracy was an integral part of the Yi Ging's criminal enterprise; its other interests and practices closely conformed to the traditional definition of organized crime, using violence to protect its lucrative markets. As head of the organization, Geng Chen presided over a flat hierarchy that coalesced around his strong leadership. In return for his supervision, Geng Chen received a share of the illegal earnings from the various criminal activi-

---

[13] Yi Ging Indictment Count 1, Sec 5, p. 7.

ties of his subordinates. He also played a hands-on role in many of the gang's enterprises.[14]

According to the indictment, Yi Ging's DVD/CD counterfeiting and money-laundering operation was quite savvy. The counterfeit goods were manufactured in China and mailed or smuggled into New York by members of the organization.[15] Gang members either delivered cash payments for the counterfeit merchandise in person or wired the money back to their co-conspirators in China.[16] Operatives were careful to carry or transmit just less than the threshold amounts of $10,000 for reporting international transport of U.S. currency and $3,000 for provision of an identification document for wire transfers.[17] The indictment alleges that proceeds from the pirated DVD/CD sales were effectively laundered, obscuring the profitability of this aspect of the Yi Ging's operation.[18] The combined proceeds from DVD/CD piracy and drug sales were estimated, for the purpose of assigning asset forfeiture, at $3 million.[19] The case is ongoing, but several of the key defendants have already pleaded guilty.[20]

The Jah Organization: Piracy and Money-Laundering Syndicate[21]

Between 2001 and 2006, the Jah organization operated out of an infamous address, 1225 Broadway, New York City, a well-known piracy haven manned by Chinese and West African merchants, many of whom were illegal aliens. The Jah organization fit seamlessly into this criminal milieu. It ran a large-scale piracy and money-laundering operation that remitted the proceeds of piracy and acted as an illegal money

---

[14] Yi Ging Indictment Count 1, Sec 4, p. 6.

[15] Yi Ging Indictment Count 22, Sec 65(a), pp. 67–68.

[16] Yi Ging Indictment Count 22, Sec 65(b), p. 68.

[17] Ibid.

[18] Yi Ging Indictment Count 1, Sec 28-30, pp. 33–35.

[19] Yi Ging Indictment Count, Forfeiture Allegation, Sec 74-75, pp. 74–75.

[20] *U.S. v. Geng Chen et al. Docket Report*, 05 Cr. 938, S.D.N.Y., All Defendants, 2005, pp. 1–74.

[21] See Appendix A, pp. 5–9, for a more detailed description of this case.

transfer service to send millions of dollars across the United States and around the world.

- **Highlight.** This case illustrates the way money-laundering activities dovetail with piracy and counterfeiting operations that are manned by undocumented workers. Jah's business was found to have laundered over $41.6 million in unregulated wire transfers and bulk cash smuggling.
- **Piracy revenues.** Analysis of the syndicate's bank account showed deposits of hundreds of thousands of dollars from the proceeds of sales of counterfeit goods. The syndicate then remitted more than $9.8 million to manufacturers in China, India, and Vietnam. The indictments seek asset forfeiture of three properties in Ohio and $26,615,628, representing the proceeds of money laundering and copyright/trademark infringement.
- **Discovery of piracy.** The Jah organization appears to have run its piracy and money-laundering businesses in parallel. The syndicate offered illicit goods and banking services from several storefronts in the 1225 Broadway complex, servicing Manhattan customers as well as mail-order clients around the United States.
- **Motivation for entry into piracy.** The Jah case study is one of vertical expansion. The skills involved in piracy and money laundering/transfer were reinforcing, and integrating the two allowed the syndicate to conduct each business effectively.
- **Role of law enforcement.** From 2001 to 2005, the NYPD exerted continuous pressure on pirates operating in the 1225 Broadway complex, through raids and seizures of counterfeit material. In 2006, the U.S. Secret Service and New York Electronic Crimes Task Force, along with the NYPD Organized Crime Investigative Division, joined the campaign against the pirates. The scales appeared to tip in favor of the authorities when U.S. Postal Service authorities helped widen the investigation, tracking the Jah syndicate's reach across several jurisdictions in Ohio and Tennessee.
- **Evidence base.** A federal indictment against Jacob Jah and four accomplices provides an in-depth look at the syndicate's illicit activity. Investigators documented piracy activity through under-

cover purchases, parcel inspections, and police raids. Money-laundering activity is detailed in remittances layered in the syndicate's four bank accounts. All of the defendants ultimately pleaded guilty.

From 2001 to 2006, large-scale piracy operations and organized criminal activity dominated a nine-story commercial building at 1225 Broadway, New York City. That notoriety led the NYPD to conduct multiple raids on the complex in 2004 and 2005, in which thousands of pirated audiovisual discs were seized.[22] One NYPD raid in particular resulted in the seizure of 68,000 pirated DVDs.[23] Police scrutiny increased dramatically in 2005 as rivalries inside the complex escalated. That summer, a shopper was killed when she was caught in the crossfire of a robbery gone wrong at one pirated-CD shop.

Jah and three associates were charged with trafficking in counterfeit goods, including fake designer handbags and unauthorized copies of motion pictures, from a store at 1225 Broadway operating under the name Djisowen, Inc.[24] The complaint stated that over the course of a two-year investigation by the U.S. Postal Service, an informant successfully purchased counterfeit handbags from the store, and postal workers in Tennessee frequently delivered large parcels from 1225 Broadway to an address in Memphis, occasionally glimpsing CDs and DVDs through holes in the packages.[25] Revenue from the sale of counterfeit goods was laundered by mailing it to co-conspirators in Columbus, Ohio, and Detroit, Michigan, who deposited the checks and cash into several bank accounts. Between March 2001 and September 2002, investigators identified more than $9,800,000 in remittances to these beneficiaries.[26]

---

[22] Jacob Jah et al. Indictment Counts 3 and 4, pp. 8–9; MPA letter to Kenneth Dreifach, Office of the Attorney General for the State of New York, August 4, 2006; MPA letter to Calvin Haddad (1225 Broadway landlord), December 12, 2005.

[23] Ibid.

[24] Ibid., pp. 8–11.

[25] Jacob Jah et al Complaint, June 3, 2004, pp. 14–16.

[26] Jacob Jah el al Indictment Count 2, pp. 4–7.

The Jah organization was also accused of carrying out unlicensed international money transfers, sometimes referred to as *hawala* (though *hawalas* can be licensed), to enable clients to avoid the scrutiny of federal authorities. According to the U.S. Attorney's Office complaint, the Jah organization transmitted more than $15 million from the Columbus accounts alone in 2003. Ultimately, Jah and six other members of the organization (two additional co-conspirators were identified and apprehended after the initial indictment) pleaded guilty to conspiracy to conduct an unlicensed money-transmitting business.[27] They also pleaded guilty to various other charges, including trafficking in false identification documents,[28] conspiracy to traffic in counterfeit goods,[29] conspiracy to criminally infringe copyrights, and money laundering.[30]

China

In sheer volume, China is possibly the largest market in the world for pirated films. Organized crime in China has a long history and is frequently associated with corrupt officials in government and the military.[31] Piracy operations in China also extend to the Chinese diaspora operating in other countries, as indicated by the cases in England, Spain, and the United States. High-profile cases offer evidence of Chinese gangs conducting piracy operations. In one unusual case, two Americans were arrested in Shanghai in April 2005 and were sentenced to prison for illegally selling $840,000 worth of pirated DVDs

---

[27] U.S. v. Jacob Jah et al. Docket Report, 1:04-Cr-00572-LAK, S.D.N.Y., All Defendants, 2005, pp. 11, 12, 15, 17, 18.

[28] Ibid., p. 17.

[29] Ibid., p. 11.

[30] Ibid., pp. 12, 22.

[31] Mark Galeotti, "Chinese crime's global reach," *Jane's Intelligence Review*, November 1, 2000; and John Hill and Ann Rogers, "Triad societies seek increased opportunities as China opens up," *Jane's Intelligence Review*, January 1, 2003.

and holding 210,000 bootleg copies in three warehouses.[32] Working together, American and Chinese law enforcement learned that the pair sold the DVDs on eBay and through a Russian website in more than two dozen countries.[33] They later were charged with and pleaded guilty to federal charges in the United States, after having been returned from prison in China.[34] On one occasion, a Chinese court sentenced a DVD pirate to life in prison.[35]

In March 2007, anti-piracy officials from China's National Anti-Piracy and Pornography Office (NAPP) and Guangzhou Cultural Task Force raided a pirate optical-disc manufacturing and storage facility in the southern Chinese city of Guangzhou.[36] It was the largest anti-piracy haul that year in China, with the seizure of 1.79 million optical discs, almost all of which were illegal—either pirated or pornographic.[37] The authorities also seized 15 machines used to erase Source Identification (SID) codes that allow investigators to determine the manufacturer of an optical disc.[38] Officials detained two men believed to be managers of the facility and extended their investigation of the illegal operation.[39]

---

[32] Zhuoqiong Wang, "American DVD piracy convict deported home," *China Daily*, September 3, 2005, available at http://www.chinadaily.com.cn/english/doc/2005-09/30/content_482005.htm (as of October 1, 2008); Jeremy Goldkorn, "Americans to be jailed in Shanghai for DVD Piracy," April 20, 2005, available at http://www.danwei.org/intellectual_property/americans_to_be_jailed_in_shan.php (as of October 1, 2008).

[33] Ibid.

[34] Ibid.

[35] "Life sentence for biggest DVD pirate," *China Economic Review*, November 24, 2006. Available at http://www.chinaeconomicreview.com/dailybriefing/2006_11_24/Life-sentence_for_biggest_DVD_pirate.html (as of October 1, 2008).

[36] Motion Picture Association, "Guangzhou Factory Raid Nets 1.79 Million Optical Discs," *Asia Pacific Anti-Piracy Update*, Issue 02-2007, available at http://www.mpa-i.org/pdf/Anti-Piracy%20Update_Issue02-2007.pdf (as of October 1, 2008); Clifford Coonan, "Chinese stage largest anti-piracy raid to date," *Variety Online*, March 27, 2007.

[37] Ibid.

[38] Ibid.

[39] Ibid.

Britain

In Britain, piracy has been nested with immigrant smuggling, as illegal migrants agree to sell pirated DVDs or are forced to do so by snakeheads to pay off their debts. One of the two case studies discussed below resulted in the tragic drowning deaths of 21 illegal immigrants.

In April 2006, British police shut down the biggest known pirate DVD factory in the country. The facility was said to be capable of producing 60,000 counterfeit DVDs per day. Three hundred titles were discovered, each selling for four to five British pounds on the street. Five Chinese nationals were arrested, and 500 burners were seized. Many films were sourced to pirates using camcorders to film new releases in the United States or illegal download sites.[40] And in November 2006, British authorities seized counterfeit Bollywood DVDs worth 5 million English pounds, the largest haul of such films to date.[41]

South London is a particular hot spot for the piracy trade. One Chinese national arrested in Britain admitted he had factories in Shanghai that manufactured DVDs and that he flew them in consignment batches of 2,000 to London's City Airport, where about 20 percent of his product was seized. He admitted to bribing film crews to get copies of new movies.[42]

Lin Liang Ren and Human Smuggling in Britain[43]
On February 5, 2004, 21 illegal Chinese immigrant cockle-pickers drowned in the rising tide of Morecambe Bay when their unlicensed

---

[40] Bob Crabtree, "Giant pirate DVD factory busted in east London," *Hexus.lifestyle*, April 7, 2006. Available at http://lifestyle.hexus.net/content/item.php?item=5276 (as of October 1, 2008).

[41] "Ealing raid nets UK's biggest haul of pirated Bollywood DVDs, (PR863)," November 2006. Available at http://www.ealing.gov.uk/press_releases/2006/november2006/pr863.html (asof October 1, 2008).

[42] Graham Johnson, "The Lord of the Stings," *Sunday Mirror*, December 14, 2003.

[43] See Appendix A, pp. 9–16, for a more detailed description of this case.

gangmaster (an English term for a contract supplier of cheap agricultural labor) forced them to work in dangerous conditions. Police identified Lian Liang Ren as the head of the syndicate and found evidence that he ran an extensive human-smuggling operation at several residences he owned. In searching these and those of three accomplices, police also found more than 4,000 counterfeit DVDs, as well as computers containing counterfeit materials.[44] Britain's National Crime Intelligence Services has since classified the case as one that highlights the "range of possible entry methods exploited by Chinese organized immigration crime groups."[45]

- **Highlight.** This case demonstrates a piracy connection to one of the most infamous incidents of illegal Chinese immigration and labor abuse in England's history. The tragedy proved to be a turning point in the government's response to the issues of illegal immigration and labor abuse, bringing new laws and enhanced enforcement on gangmasters, as well as raising public awareness of the peril of snakehead gangs.
- **Piracy revenue.** Piracy revenue was a secondary but important part of Lin Liang Ren's operation. The commercial scale of operations showed a significant investment in equipment and blank media.
- **Discovery of piracy.** As authorities learned of Lin's syndicate only after the drowning tragedy, there was no surveillance or intelligence about how he entered into piracy.

---

[44] The fact that the cockle-pickers had cell phones suggests that they were not being held in captivity in the same way that victims of trafficking usually are. See Sheldon Zhang, *Chinese Human Smuggling Organizations: Families, Social Networks, and Cultural Imperatives,* Stanford, CA: Stanford University Press, 2008; Ko-Lin Chin, *Smuggled Chinese: Clandestine Immigration to the United States,* Philadelphia, PA: Temple University Press, 1999.

[45] National Criminal Intelligence Service (United Kingdom), *UK Threat Assessment: The Threat from Serious and Organized Crime 2004/5–2005/6,* p. 27. Available at http://www.ncis.gov.uk/ukta/2004/UKTA_2004-05_2005-06.pdf (as of August 13, 2008).

- **Motivation for entry into piracy.** This is another case of vertical expansion, for Lin's piracy operation was a direct extension of the gang's primary activity, human smuggling. By expanding into piracy, Lin Liang Ren was able to capture additional profits from the labor he had at his disposal.
- **Role of law enforcement.** Experienced police identified the piracy operation they uncovered. Prosecutors successfully convicted Lin's accomplice of 11 counts of copyright infringement.
- **Evidence base.** The evidence base comprises the court proceedings and press accounts, which provide vivid details of the drowning tragedy and the national response that followed.

When the 21 Chinese immigrants drowned, the ensuing death inquiry quickly snowballed into one of the largest criminal investigations in the history of the Lancashire constabulary.[46] Operation Lund, as the investigation was called, uncovered evidence of human smuggling, exploitation, and criminal negligence by a party also engaged in large-scale DVD counterfeiting. Illegal Chinese immigrants are said to be the main source of cheap labor in a profitable "shadow industry" of cockle-picking in Britain.[47] Like many other menial jobs, cockle-picking in Morecambe Bay is both arduous and potentially perilous. Within the space of an hour, the tidewater can move from more than five miles out in the bay to 30 feet deep at the shoreline.[48]

On this occasion, the illegal Chinese immigrants kept harvesting cockles into the night to repay debts to their human smugglers, even though they were unfamiliar with the terrain. They were caught when

---

[46] "Government criticized over cockling deaths," *Guardian Unlimited*, March 24, 2006.

[47] Hsai-hung Pai, "I'm illegal, so what can I do?" *The Guardian*, February 9, 2004.

[48] "Trial over deaths of Chinese cockle pickers starts in Britain," *People's Daily Online*, September 20, 2005.

the waters rose behind them, cutting off access to the shore.[49] Many of the victims used mobile phones to make calls to loved ones in China as death approached, and the transcripts of those conversations roiled the British press for days. One headline read: "I am up to my chest in water. Tell my family to pray for me . . . I am dying."[50]

The hapless Chinese immigrants had been in the employ of a man named Lin Liang Ren and his two familial associates, Zhao Xiao Qing (Lin's girlfriend) and Lin Mu Yong (his cousin), who forced them to work illegally for the Spanish multinational, Dani, to pay off their debts. Media accounts of the investigation and trial frequently referred to Lin Liang Ren as a "gangmaster."[51]

Lin Liang Ren was ultimately charged with 21 counts of manslaughter, conspiracy to violate immigration laws, and conspiracy to pervert the course of justice through lies, witness intimidation, and destruction of evidence. While no evidence was found to explicitly implicate Lin Liang Ren in DVD piracy,[52] police discovered tens of thousands of counterfeit DVDs, disc copiers, and high-end printers in a search of Lin Mu Yong's residence. Counterfeit DVDs like those found at the residence were being sold by Chinese illegal immigrants in the area. These circumstances suggest that the immigrant cockle-pickers were recruited to also assist in the manufacture and sale of the counterfeit DVDs. Lin Mu Yong was charged with both immigration

---

[49] Ian Herbert, "Gangmaster guilty of manslaughter after 21 Chinese cocklers were engulfed by tide," *The Independent UK*, March 25, 2006. Available at http://www.independent. co.uk/news/uk/crime/gangmaster-guilty-of-manslaughter-after-21-chinese-cocklers-were-engulfed-by-tide-471318.html (as of October 10, 2008).

[50] Richard Spencer, "I am up to my chest in water. Tell my family to pray for me . . . I am dying," *Daily Telegraph*, February 11, 2004.

[51] Felicity Lawrence, "The new landless labourers," *The Guardian*, May 17, 2003.

[52] The following details are from Mick Gradwell, Senior Investigating Officer of the Lancashire Constabulary, "Operation Lund," email to Carl Matthies, RAND Corporation, Santa Monica, CA, December 3, 2007.

and trademark offenses.[53] Both Lin Liang Ren and Lin Mu Yong were convicted, along with Zhao Xiao Qing.[54]

Lotus Trading Company[55]

In April 2003, Britain's Metropolitan Police Service (MPS) arrested Justin Ng when he arrived at a London UPS office to pick up a package of pirated DVDs. Raiding Ng's residence, police found an extensive DVD import/export business that brought pirated DVDs from Malaysia and distributed them all over London. Workers arrested at the Ng's residence confirmed that Ng was using illegal Chinese immigrant labor to run his operation. Ng's journal, found at the scene of the crime, provided extensive information on a human-smuggling ring in which victims paid off their debts by selling pirated DVDs.

- **Highlight.** This case is one example of how investigating piracy led authorities to still more serious crimes, human smuggling or trafficking.
- **Piracy revenue.** Piracy was a primary revenue source for Ng's syndicate. The journal details the costs for piracy shipments from Malaysia and provides a breakdown of how each smuggling victim accumulated tens of thousands of dollars of debt.
- **Discovery of piracy.** The chronology of short message service (SMS) texts Ng logged in his journal indicates that he entered into piracy from the beginning and that piracy was tightly linked with his human-smuggling operations.
- **Motivation for entry into piracy.** This is yet another case of vertical expansion as a natural complement to human smuggling.
- **Role of law enforcement.** The MPS acted swiftly to apprehend Ng and raid his apartment after being tipped off by UPS. How-

---

[53] *Certificate of Conviction, Case No T20050022, def. Mu Yong Lin,* and *Certificate of Conviction, Case No T20047476-2, def. Mu Yong Lin,* Preston Crown Court, England, issued December 4, 2007.

[54] Ibid.; *Certificate of Conviction, Case No. T20047476-1, def. Liang Ren Lin,* Preston Crown Court, England, issued December 4, 2007; *Certificate of Conviction, Case No T20047476-3, def. Xiao Qing Zhao,* Preston Crown Court, England, issued December 4, 2007.

[55] See Appendix A, pp. 16–18, for a more detailed description of this case.

ever, when released on bail, Ng and the other defendants disappeared, forcing the MPS and UK Immigration Services to suspended further investigation.

- **Evidence base.** Although there was no trial or conviction, Ng's journal still provides detailed evidence. This primary document is supplemented by police and industry members' accounts of the raid.

What began as simple interdiction of pirated DVDs led to the discovery of a complex human-smuggling operation whose clients repaid their debts by selling the counterfeit goods.[56] In April 2003, the MPS arrested a Singaporean named Justin Ng (who was carrying £4,000 in cash in his pocket) and a Chinese associate named Ming Hua when they arrived at a UPS office to pick up a package of pirated DVDs. The subsequent search of Ng's apartment by MPS uncovered an extensive DVD import/export business with the name Lotus Trading Company that brought pirated DVDs into Britain from Malaysia. A map of the distribution network is shown in Figure 4.1. Most important, police confiscated Ng's journal, which was conveniently filled with details of his criminal enterprise.[57]

Entries in the journal implicated Ng as a leader in a network that smuggled people as well as counterfeit DVDs. One page with the heading "China Snakehead" (in Chinese) tallies expenses for the transport of a "client" from Beijing to England by way of France, Africa, and Spain, an itinerary that is consistent with one of the major human-smuggling routes identified in the Serious Organized Crime Agency's 2006/07 Threat Assessment.[58] Unfortunately, all those arrested in con-

---

[56] Many of the details of this case are based on the recollections of Mick Buchan, who was a Senior Investigator with the United Kingdom Federation Against Copyright Theft (UKFACT) at the time of Ng's arrest, and on documents possessed by UKFACT that were made available to RAND.

[57] Interview with Mick Buchan, UKFACT, by Jonathan Dotan, an organized-crime consultant to the MPA, May 10, 2007.

[58] "Lotus Trading Co. Importer Exporter," journal received by MPA from investigators, May 10, 2007, p. 13; The Home Office, "Serious Organized Crime Agency's 2006/2007 Threat Assessment," London, 2006.

Figure 4.1
Lotus Trading Company Distribution Network

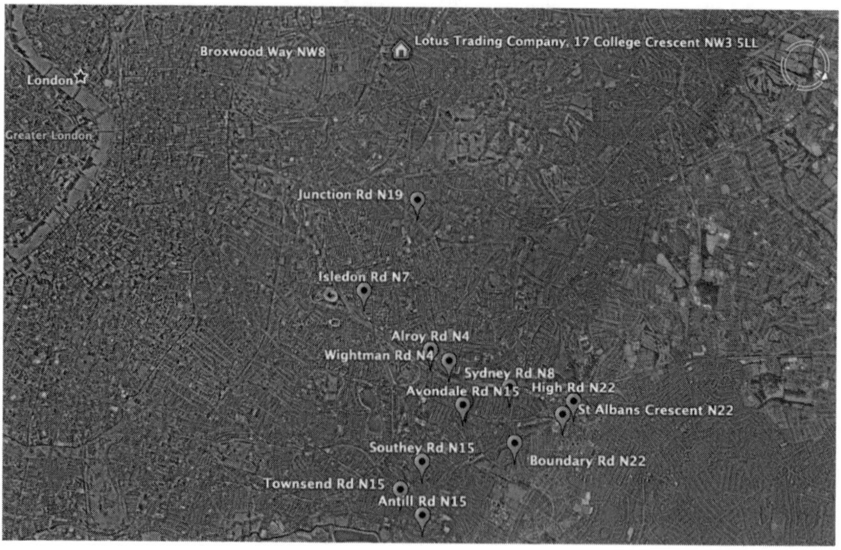

RAND *MG742-4.1*

nection with the case made bail and immediately disappeared, taking with them any hope of a prosecution for immigration and trademark offenses, at least in the near future.

Spain

Since 2000, Spain has seen an explosion of illegal Chinese immigration, most of the immigrants coming from the underdeveloped agricultural province of Zhejiang.[59] Police estimate that the number could be as high as 50,000, of whom with almost one-third are performing virtual slave labor in workshops run by local and international Chinese gangs. The following case provides an in-depth look at a sophisti-

---

[59] Glenn E. Curtis et al., *Transnational Activities of Chinese Crime Organizations*, Washington, D.C.: Congressional Research Service, April 2003, p. 18.

cated piracy ring, spread over 23 locations in and around Madrid and manned by smuggled humans working to pay off their debts.

Operations Katana and Sudoku: Chinese Human Smuggling[60]

- **Highlight.** The piracy ring in this case used the same modus operandi as the Chinese gangs in England profiled above. It confirms a pattern of piracy and human smuggling seen in the Chinese diaspora communities in Europe and elsewhere in the world.
- **Piracy revenue.** Piracy was the primary source of revenue for the gang. Operations could reportedly reproduce and sell more than 1.3 million DVDs and CDs a month, worth an estimated $18 million in damages to the film and music industries.
- **Discovery of piracy.** The gang engaged in piracy from the beginning; its human-smuggling operation facilitated that piracy by providing a source of cheap labor.
- **Motivation for entry into piracy.** Another case of vertical expansion, this case, along with the British cases above, confirms that piracy can be an important component in the set of crimes associated with human smuggling.
- **Role of law enforcement.** Spanish police closely monitored the gang for three months to identify its leaders and then coordinated an impressive 23-location raid across two cities.
- **Evidence base.** The evidence base comprises nearly 50 pages of police records supplemented by interviews with police officers and press reports.

On October 28, 2005, Spanish police arrested 69 illegal Chinese immigrants in 23 raids in two sting operations across Madrid and Leganés.[61] The sting operations, named Operations Katana and Sudoku, netted 18 duplicators with a total of 161 burners, two CPUs,

---

[60] See Appendix A, pp.18–21, for a more detailed description of this case.

[61] "Wave of arrests in Spain over fake DVDs, CDs," *Agence France-Presse*, October 27, 2005; Operations Katana and Sudoku police records, received from the Spanish National Unit Against Organized Crime, December 1, 2006.

five photocopiers, 54,426 CD-Rs, 22,985 blank CD-Rs, and 1,645 DVD-Rs.[62] Police surveillance leading up to the arrests revealed a piracy ring led by two Chinese nationals who brought illegal workers from Zhejiang province to work for the piracy gang.[63] Police concluded that of the 69 arrested in the two operations, 26 were members of the gang, and seven had previous records for counterfeiting.[64] It was, in the words of the Spanish police report, "one of the most structured organizations dedicated to this activity yet discovered in Europe . . ., mutating in response to setbacks it suffered at the hands of police."

The gang's operations bore the signs of human smuggling, and, as Justin Ng's journal detailed in the British case, Spain is a key transit country for illegal Chinese nationals awaiting work in cities in Europe and as far away as Canada, South Africa, and Mexico.[65] While in transit, victims often have to stay at an intermediate site to liquidate their debts before they reach their final destination.[66] Many work in deplorable conditions in clandestine textile workshops, restaurants, or, as in this case, by producing and selling pirated films and music.[67]

Raids on Chinese Diaspora Organized Crime in 2008

While the 2005 police operations were a success, Chinese involvement in piracy did not abate. On March 12, 2008, Spanish police raided three warehouses and arrested six Chinese nationals, alleged members

---

[62] Operations Katana and Sudoku police records, 2006.

[63] "Wave of arrests in Spain over fake DVDs, CDs," 2005; Operations Katana and Sudoku police records, 2006.

[64] Ibid.

[65] Naomi Schwarz, "Enforcement Fails to Slow Illegal West African Immigration to Europe," *VOA News*, December 18, 2007. Available at http://www.voanews.com/english/archive/2007-12/2007-12-18-voa56.cfm?CFID=25534758&CFTOKEN=74254461 (as of August 18, 2008).

[66] Dr. Carlos Resa Nestares, "Transnational Organized Crime Activities in Spain: Structural Factors Explaining Its Penetration," Madrid: University of Madrid, Applied Economics Working Paper, February 27, 2001. Available at http://www.uam.es/personal_pdi/economicas/cresa/text9.html (as of August 13, 2008)

[67] Foreign Broadcast Information Service, "Chinese immigration ring smashed in Spain," translated from *Madrid EFE*, FBIS Document ID EUP2002101500032, October 15, 2002.

of an unidentified organized-crime ring, in what was called the country's "biggest crackdown on illegal street sales."[68] The crime organization had many similarities to the one taken down in the Katana and Sudoku operations and reportedly had the capacity to produce a staggering 80,000 pirated DVDs and CDs per day.

Arrests came after Spain's Intellectual Property Brigade discovered 20 recording towers, 155,000 blank and pirated CDs and DVDs, and 240 duplication machines in the three raided warehouses in Leganés and southern Madrid and a duplication center in Arganda del Rey, just outside Madrid. Police also found "master copies" of movies illegally recorded in theaters, some of which had not yet been released in Spain. According to police, the revenues from these operations were estimated to total 240,000 (approximately $370,000) per day.[69]

On June 2, 2008, Spanish police conducted the largest street-piracy operation in Spanish history, and perhaps the largest to date in Europe, when over 400 officers raided an organized piracy ring run by Chinese nationals in 10 different cities, arresting 32 persons.[70] Seizures included over 162,000 recorded DVD-Rs and 506 burners, as well as 144,000 music CDs, nearly 500,000 unrecorded discs, and related printing and packaging equipment. The equipment seized allowed the piracy organization to produce up to 150,000 discs per day. In fact, during the investigation, police monitoring of courier shipments to cities outside Madrid showed that the organization sent out more than three tons of product in April and May alone.

According to law enforcement, the organized piracy ring, run by gang leaders Zheng Rongliang and Lupeng Yang, were exploiting Chinese immigrant workers whom they illegally smuggled to Spain,

---

[68] "Spanish police report biggest raid ever against audiovisual bootlegging," *Associated Press Worldstream*, March 12, 2008. See also Emiliano de Pablos and John Hopewell, "Spain cracks down on pirates," *Variety*, March 13, 2008.

[69] de Pablos and Hopewell, 2008; Pamela Rolfe, "Madrid CD/DVD Pirate Ring Busted," *Hollywood Reporter*, March 13, 2008.

[70] All the details in this paragraph are from "Desarticulación de un Grupo Organizado de Ciudadanos Chinos," Official Press Release of the Ministerio del Interior & Dirección General de la Policía y de G.C. Comisaría General de Policía Judicial, June 2, 2008.

forcing them to pay off their travel debt under harsh conditions for a period of three to four years.[71]

Italy

The Camorra is an organized-crime network with a large international reach and stakes in construction, high fashion, illicit drugs, and toxic-waste disposal.[72] Centered in Naples and known by insiders as "the System," the Camorra afflicts cities and villages along the Neapolitan coast and is the major reason for Campania, for instance, having the highest murder rate in all of Europe and cancer levels that have sky-rocketed in recent years.[73] Huge cargoes of Chinese goods are shipped to Naples and then quickly distributed, unchecked, across Europe. The Camorra controls thousands of Chinese factories contracted to manu-facture fashion goods, legally and illegally, for distribution around the world.[74] Heedless handling of toxic waste by the gang is causing devas-tating pollution, not only in Naples but also as far away as China and Somalia.

Camorra: Naples-Based Transnational Mafia Syndicate[75]
As a federation of 20 active Mafia clans, the Camorra is believed by authorities to have more than 8,000 "made members" belonging to more than 100 crime families, and more than 120,000 foot soldiers, associates, and sympathizers. The Camorra's illicit revenues are esti-mated to exceed $33 billion a year and are produced by narcotics,

---

[71] Ibid.

[72] Philip Willan, "Camorra factions vie for control of Naples drugs market," *Jane's Intelligence Review*, February 1, 2005.

[73] For a gripping first-person account, see Roberto Saviano, *Gomorrah: A Personal Journey into the Violent International Empire of Naples' Organized Crime System,* trans. Virginia Jewiss, New York: Farrar, Straus and Giroux, 2007.

[74] Philip Willan, "Police crack down on Camorra's counterfeit goods trade," *Jane's Intelligence Review*, March 7, 2005.

[75] See Appendix A, pp. 21–26, for a more detailed description of this case.

arms, and human trafficking, along with illegal refuse disposal, cigarette smuggling, extortion, prostitution, loan-sharking, and, increasingly, counterfeiting and piracy.[76]

- **Highlight.** The Camorra's "Alleanza di Secondigliano" involvement in piracy spans more than 20 years, making it one of the longest-standing connections between piracy and organized crime in a single organization.
- **Piracy revenue.** Anti-Mafia magistrates confiscated an estimated $780 million worth of counterfeit goods (not only DVDs) from the Camorra in 2003 and 2004, seizing 68 Camorra-linked counterfeiting companies in 2004 alone.
- **Discovery of piracy.** Recent testimony by a convicted Camorra leader indicates that the Mafia's leadership made a deliberate decision to get into videocassette and CD piracy in 1986, entrusting a large part of the business to the Frattasio family, which has remained active since the beginning of the operation and whose members were picked up in piracy sweeps as recently as 2004.
- **Motivation for entry into piracy.** This case is one of horizontal expansion. The Camorra expanded into piracy and counterfeiting to diversify a portfolio of long-standing criminal business enterprises; it did so by opening its own manufacturing businesses or, in some instances, partnering with other organized-crime groups.
- **Role of law enforcement.** After November 2004, the Direzione Nazionale Antimafia (DNA), the Guardia di Finanza (GdF), and the Servizio Centrale di Investigazione sulla Criminalità Organizzata (SCICO) heightened their efforts to stem the Camorra's profits from counterfeiting. Their efforts led to arrests in Canada, France, Spain, Belgium, and Germany. In 2006, an exhaustive analysis of GdF and SCICO records singled out 31 Mafia members of special investigative importance known to be involved in counterfeiting and piracy.
- **Evidence base.** The evidence for this case is built on testimony submitted in two major trials that provide an unprecedented look

---

[76] Willan, "Police crack down on Camorra's counterfeit goods trade," 2005.

at the 20-year history of the Camorra's involvement in counterfeiting and piracy. Additional evidence, in the form of police reports and intelligence analysis, was provided through cooperation with anti-Mafia magistrates.

For the Camorra, counterfeiting further diversified an impressive portfolio of criminal enterprises that included drug dealing, extortion, prostitution, loan-sharking, arms and cigarette smuggling, human smuggling, and illegal refuse disposal.[77] As of 2005, the Camorra's revenue from drugs was estimated at $21 billion annually; the estimated annual gross from all activities was estimated at $33 billion.[78] Experts believe the Camorra's expanding role in counterfeiting is part of the group's attempt to reinvent itself as less evil and more a provider of coveted goods and services, one with a lower profile for law enforcement.[79] An important aspect of the Camorra's new business model, with regard to counterfeiting in particular, has been increased cooperation with the Taiwanese and Chinese triads.[80]

As part of stepped-up enforcement against the Camorra's DVD piracy by the DNA, GdF, and SCICO, an operation dubbed "Tarantella," conducted in 2002, probed Camorra-owned businesses in the Campania region and learned that the Camorra's modus operandi was to fake copyright certificates to trick legitimate mastering companies and duplicators into producing copies—thus obtaining especially good copies.[81] Operation Tarantella provided the intelligence foundation for Operation Jolly Roger, a more expansive investigation that made use of surveillance and forensic analysis of confiscated DVDs.

---

[77] Alison Jamieson, "Italy's gangs change their tactics," *Jane's Intelligence Review*, November 21, 2001.

[78] Willan, "Camorra factions vie for control of Naples drug market," 2005.

[79] Willan, "Police crack down on Camorra's counterfeit goods trade," 2005.

[80] *Counterfeiting: A Global Spread, A Global Threat*, Report of the Anti-Human Trafficking and Emerging Crimes Unit of the United Nations Interregional Crime and Justice Research Institute (UNICRI), December 2007, p. 120.

[81] Luciano Daffarra, report on Camorra Piracy for MPA, November 29, 2006.

Hong Kong[82]

Hong Kong's two major triad societies, the Wo Shing Wo (WSW) and the Sun Yee On, are a bifurcated network of high-level white-collar criminals and a confederation of low-level street gangs that engage in core illicit businesses: narcotics trafficking, protection rackets, gambling, loan-sharking, prostitution, human smuggling, and counterfeiting.[83] The WSW triad, now the dominant organization on the streets of Hong Kong, is estimated to have more than 120,000 members and is believed to be the most diversified in its criminal activities.[84] WSW gangs act independently but maintain the appearance of a menacing unified front through rituals and customs.[85] Hence, many criminals seek affiliation with WSW and other triads to project intimidating criminal credentials.

- **Highlight.** When effective IPR enforcement drove many amateur pirates out of business, Hong Kong's two major triad societies, the Sun Yee On and the Wo Shing Wo, expanded their role in piracy to fill the void. This case demonstrates how hardened organized-crime groups not only survive but can expand in the face of serious IPR enforcement.
- **Piracy revenue.** Triads are believed to dominate the $25-million-a-year pirate disc trade that operates in Kowloon. Each year, Hong Kong authorities have seized pirated goods worth millions of dollars as part of a comprehensive approach to bankrupting triad businesses. In the past two years, prosecutors have applied to freeze more than $2 million in triad assets.

---

[82] See Appendix A, pp. 26–38, for a more detailed description of this case.

[83] "Profile of the Wo Shing Wo," *Next Magazine,* February 20, 2003. There is a debate among experts over how much of Chinese organized crime involves triads and how much is based on *guanxi* (personalized networks of influence). Some crimes attributed to the triads probably reflect individual or small-group entrepreneurship. See Yiu Kong Chu, *The Triads as Business,* London: Routledge, 2000.

[84] Yi Kong Chu, "Hong Kong Triads after 1997," *Trends in Organized Crime,* Vol. 8, No. 3, March 2005, pp. 5–12.

[85] Hill and Rogers, 2003.

- **Discovery of piracy.** The triads moved easily into piracy from running powerful extortion rackets in the Hong Kong film industry since the early 1980s. The WSW triad built its core strength on its piracy business and used the proceeds to finance operations in narcotics and prostitution.
- **Motivation for entry into piracy.** This case exhibits consolidation and horizontal expansion. The triads moved into piracy to consolidate territorial control over their rackets in Kowloon, but piracy also became an additional revenue stream in a host of other serious crimes.
- **Role of law enforcement.** Hong Kong Customs and Excise runs one of the best anti-piracy programs in Asia. It joins with the Organized Crime and Triad Bureau to run dedicated task forces that target the leaders of larger triad-run piracy rings. The squads comprise not only customs officers but also members of the intelligence bureau and the financial investigation group. Their efforts have been augmented through enhanced surveillance and prosecutorial powers authorized by organized-crime ordinances that include piracy offenses as predicate crimes.
- **Evidence base.** The evidence for this case is drawn from police reports from major anti-triad operations and evidence presented in prosecutions under the Hong Kong Organized and Serious Crime Ordinance (OSCO). These materials were supplemented by meetings with customs authorities and members of the Organized Crime and Triad Bureau.

Since the 1980s, Hong Kong has been a thriving shopping destination for counterfeit products of all types—from apparel, fashion accessories, and watches to counterfeit pirate films.[86] The arrival of the VCD and DVD formats resulted in an explosion of high-quality piracy in the late 1990s. This digital revolution swelled into a perfect storm for pirate activity as the Asia economic turmoil pushed cash-strapped consumers to turn more readily to cheap counterfeits.

---

[86] Connie Ling, "Asia's Entertainment Industries Fight to Cope with VCD Piracy," *Wall Street Journal Interactive Edition*, March 29, 1999.

While it was widely reported that Hong Kong's powerful underworld societies, known as triads, were responsible for the counterfeit DVD market, their role was somewhat obscured by the prevalence of hundreds of amateur and semiprofessional pirate entrepreneurs.[87] In the early days, these pirates, who had no criminal backgrounds, flooded the market with goods and operated with relative impunity—as did their mainland counterparts in Beijing and Shanghai. As the Hong Kong Customs and Excise (HKC&E) authorities ramped up their efforts to curb piracy around the turn of the millennium, most of these amateurs were driven from the market. The fiscal risk and social stigma of an arrest seemed to outweigh the benefits for typical "mom-and-pop" operators.

Thus, when HKC&E forced the closure of almost 1,000 pirate disc outlets (see Figure 4.2), the role of the triads began to appear more clearly, and in some cases, these gangs expanded to fill the void. A hardened group of 80 to 100 stores have endured repeated HKC&E raids as a tolerable cost of doing business. [88] These operations are typically manned by local drug addicts and mainland-Chinese illegal immigrants who receive instructions from remote middlemen on where and how to push product. Syndicate chiefs therefore continue to elude capture through the use of these "ghosts" or the names of drug addicts on leases.[89]

Enforcement action in 2003–2006 focused on the WSW triad. Authorities state that the objective of these operations was to deal a severe blow to triad financial resources.[90] By stemming the flow of cash from piracy and other businesses, police aimed to eliminate one possible source of funding for large-scale drug production, people-smuggling, and other major criminal enterprises.[91] For example,

---

[87] The details in this paragraph are from a briefing presented by Albert Chan, Chief, Hong Kong Customs and Excise Special Task Force, August 17, 2005.

[88] Ibid.

[89] Peter Michael, "Triads milk $1.7m a day from porn," *South China Morning Post,* November 3, 2004.

[90] "Police break up two syndicates pirating discs," *South China Morning Post*, June 30, 2005, p. 4.

[91] Michael, 2004.

Figure 4.2
HKC&E Pirate Retail Store Closures, 1999–2004

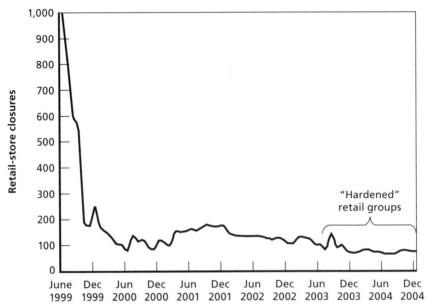

SOURCE: Hong Kong Customs and Excise internal records.
RAND *MG742-4.2*

Operation Touchdown in 2007 disrupted a film piracy syndicate backed by the Sun Yee On triad, resulting in the arrest of two alleged key members, who were charged with copyright and OSCO offenses.[92] Operation Glacier in 2005 brought down a major organized-crime syndicate engaged in large-scale DVD piracy and led by a mid-ranking member of the WSW triad.[93] In Operation Sunrise in 2004, which included intelligence cooperation with Macau and Guangdong,

---

[92] "HK Customs smashes piracy syndicate," *Hong Kong Customs and Excise Press Release*, February 15, 2007.

[93] "Triad-run Piracy Syndicate Smashed by Customs," *Hong Kong Customs and Excise Press Release*, August 5, 2005; Chan Mei Mei and Tao King Tak, "Customs chase after the four kingpins of pirates," *East Week*, October 6, 2004.

officers raided more than 2,000 locations, arresting 802 men and 767 women.[94]

Malaysia

As law enforcement in China and Hong Kong began to crack down aggressively on burning labs and began arresting organized-crime bosses as well as low-level front men in the 1990s, Malaysia became a major center for the production and distribution of pirated films.[95] Many of the counterfeiting operations in Malaysia, including the United Bamboo Gang, which has infiltrated virtually every aspect of society in the island state, from politics to the real estate and construction industry to the entertainment and tourism industry, are said to have ties to organized crime in Taiwan.[96]

In a country with a population of only 25 million, Malaysia's 126 production lines are calculated to produce more than 441 million discs per year.[97] Only about one-tenth of this capacity is estimated to service a legitimate domestic market, and part of the balance feeds the domestic black market of pirated films. Illegal burning labs have been found in Serembum, Niali, and Sengai Buluh.

Since Malaysia is a major trading and shipping center, by both regional and world standards, it is easy to ship out tens of thousands of counterfeit DVDs among the thousands of containers that go through the country's Port Klang daily or via air cargo from the Kuala Lumpur international airport. Not every container or air package is checked—

---

[94] Peter Michael, "Huge triad sweep fails to snare big bosses," *South China Morning Post,* September 10, 2004.

[95] "Triad-run Piracy Syndicate Smashed by Customs," 2005; Chan Mei Mei and Tao King Tak, 2004.

[96] U.S. General Accounting Office, "Nontraditional Organized Crime: Law Enforcement Officials' Perspectives on Five Criminal Groups," Report number OSI-18-19, 1989. Available at http://archive.gao.gov/d26t7/139919.pdf (as of September 24, 2008).

[97] International Intellectual Property Alliance, *Special 201 Report: Malaysia*, 2005. Available at http://www.iipa.com/rbc/2005/2005SPEC301MALAYSIArev.pdf (as of August 13, 2008).

trying to check every container or package would be unrealistic given the time constraints of global logistics—and even if some counterfeit DVDs are detected and confiscated, many more are likely to make it through to their final destinations, generating profits high enough to cover the losses. As the British case demonstrated, one criminal gang sourced its counterfeit pirated films for sale in the streets and pubs of London from air-delivered packages from Malaysia.

Ang Bin Hoey Triad[98]

This triad comprises a network of more than a hundred street gangs with an estimated 11,000 members who operate in Kuala Lumpur and Klang Valley.[99] By the end of the 1990s, Khoo Te Yam emerged as the *de facto* dragonhead (leader) of the triad and within a few years amassed an empire of 130 legitimate businesses under his name. Using his lieutenants as nominees, he is alleged to have further controlled more than 1,000 companies, many of them illicit, including several piracy factories. Under Khoo Te Yam's leadership, astreet gang called Gang 21 dominated the extortion rackets in Kuala Lumpur, including those that violently regulated the city's DVD/VCD piracy markets.

- **Highlight.** The case of the Ang Bin Hoey triad demonstrates how piracy operations fit easily into a traditional, hierarchical organized-crime structure.
- **Piracy revenue.** The triad profited from piracy primarily through the extortion of vendors in Kuala Lumpur. While this revenue was only a small part of Khoo Te Yam's empire, the piracy racket was attractive enough to spark violence among rival gangs looking to control markets in Petaling Jaya.
- **Discovery of Piracy.** The triad's piracy operations developed alongside its other criminal enterprises. When the pirate market became oversupplied after 2001, several street gangs under the

---

[98] See Appendix A, pp. 40–47, for a more detailed description of this case.

[99] "Crime lord's 10-year reign comes to an end," *Malay Mail*, May 26, 2004; V. Vasudevan, "Three main groups run hundreds of gangs," *New Straits Times*, July 19, 2007.

triad's control (Gangs 21, 24, and 360) stepped in to stabilize the market.

- **Motivation for entry into piracy.** This is another example of both consolidation and horizontal expansion. At the street level, the triad's gangs consolidated its power over territory across Kuala Lumpur in part by including profitable piracy markets among its rackets. Khoo Te Yam expanded horizontally into piracy manufacturing as part of 1,000 companies he is alleged to have controlled across both licit and illicit markets.
- **Role of law enforcement.** Enforcement of anti-piracy laws in Malaysia is handled by the Ministry of Domestic Trade and Consumer Affairs (MDTCA), which employs dedicated officers to handle piracy cases alongside local police officers. Over the years, enforcement has been met with violence and intimidation from pirates, culminating with death threats against the MDTCA Minister Tan Sri Muhyiddin Yassin. As in Hong Kong, the role of the triads in piracy became more evident as anti-piracy efforts became more effective, driving out the smaller, more vulnerable operators.
- **Evidence base.** In 2004, the Inspector General of Police relaunched Operation Copperhead, which resulted in Khoo's arrest and yielded the intelligence on which this case is grounded. Information on the operations was compiled from numerous press reports and verified by interviews with law enforcement.

Secret societies in Malaysia sprung up in the late 19th century as satellites of the Singaporean triads and made steep inroads into the migrant-labor Chinese populations that came to work in the country's tin mines.[100] Of the four triads that dominated the Malaya peninsula during British rule, the Wah Kee (strongest during the 1980s) and Ang Bin Hoey (dominant in present-day Kuala Lumpur) have survived.[101]

---

[100] Lau Fong Mak, *The Sociology of Secret Societies: A Study of Chinese Secret Societies in Singapore and Peninsular Malaysia,* Kuala Lumpur: Oxford University Press, 1981.

[101] T. N. Harper, *The End of Empire and the Making of Malaya*, Cambridge, UK: Cambridge University Press, 2001, pp. 112, 159, 187.

Their businesses run the gamut of vice, from narcotics trafficking and gambling to human smuggling and, most pervasively, racketeering.[102] In 2004, the newly appointed Malaysian Inspector General of Police renewed efforts to fight organized crime by dedicating more resources to Operation Copperhead, originally begun in 1998.[103] More than 50 major organized criminals, including crime bosses and senior lieutenants from the Ang Bin Hoey Triad, were arrested that year. In the course of investigations, many details emerged about the triad's more than 1,000 businesses, including its control over piracy operations in Kuala Lumpur.[104] The Malaysian government singled out the dragonhead of the Ang Bin Hoey triad, Tee Yam (aka Khoo Tee Yam), as its first priority.[105] His arrest in March 2004 and subsequent conviction were landmark events that signaled a turning point in the government's campaign.[106]

According to police, Khoo Tee Yam delegated responsibility for the various facets of his criminal conglomerate to three Gang 21 lieutenants, one of whom, Lim Beng Hian, allegedly ran the syndicate's legitimate face—discotheques and karaoke bars, which doubled as venues for prostitution and drug dealing—as well as the gang's VCD piracy operation.[107] Lim Beng Hian moved into optical-disc piracy by setting up several factories in Serenbum/Niali and Sungai Buluh during 2000–2003, all of which were raided by the MDTCA.[108] His foot soldiers regulated, often violently, a massive VCD protection racket

---

[102] "Police Closing in on Crime Lord," *New Straits Times,* May 12, 2004.

[103] "Police keeping tabs on 450 gangsters in city," *Malay Mail,* May 18, 2002, p. 2.

[104] "Crime lord's 10-year reign comes to an end," 2004.

[105] "Triad boss sent to detention center," *New Straits Times,* May 25, 2004.

[106] Ibid.

[107] Lionel Morais and Timothy Leonard, "Cops hunt for 3 trusted lieutenants," *Malay Mail,* April 27, 2004, p. 2.

[108] Jonathan Dotan, interviews with Serious Crime Division of Malaysian Police, August 1, 2005.

in Petaling Jaya at the height of the area's piracy trade in 2001.[109] Lim Beng Hian is still at large.[110]

The Bottom Line

These cases clearly demonstrate that piracy is not a victimless crime: All these organized criminal syndicates engaged in other, often more serious crimes. And in none of the cases was the threat of violence very far from the surface. The cases illustrate several other key points. The size of the gangs varied enormously. The fact that one of the most horrific crimes, the drowning of the Chinese in Morecambe Bay, was the work of a gang of three is testimony to how much damage small groups can do in today's connected world.[111] Few obstacles stood in the way of the criminal groups entering into the manufacturing of pirated films. The cases demonstrate that, as compared to other forms of counterfeiting, such as textiles or pharmaceuticals, piracy's low barrier to entry allows relatively easy access to the black market for both retailers and manufacturers.

---

[109] Eddie Chua, "VCD gangs war in SS2," *Malay Mail,* December 14, 1999, p. 2.

[110] Jonathan Dotan, interviews with Serious Crime Division of Malaysian Police, August 1, 2005.

[111] Zhang uses the concept of the "dyadic cartwheel network" to explain how and why freelance operators instead of traditional crime syndicates have come to dominate the human-smuggling enterprise. See Sheldon Zhang, *Chinese Human Smuggling Organizations: Families, Social Networks, and Cultural Imperatives,* Stanford, CA: Stanford University Press, 2008.

CHAPTER FIVE

Terrorism and Film Piracy: Known Cases

In three of our case studies, the trail of film piracy leads to terrorism, as terrorist groups either engaged in piracy to fund their terror or received support from sympathizers who engaged in crime. The criminal groups in the case studies and their criminal activities are summarized in Table 5.1. The cases suggest that the connection between piracy and terrorism may be stronger than previously believed. Further study is warranted to confirm the extent and strength of that connection.

Earlier RAND research on the growing convergence of crime and terrorism networks identified counterfeiting as one of several activities groups used to tap "locally available sources of revenue" to maintain

Table 5.1
Overview of Case Studies of Terrorism and Piracy

Organized-Crime Group	Base Location	Film Piracy	Counterfeiting	Racketeering	Human Smuggling	Money Laundering / Illegal Money Transfer Service	Illegal Gambling	Loan Sharking	Narcotics Trafficking	Prostitution	Weapon Trafficking	Contract Killing	Document Forgery Services
Barakat Network	Paraguay	x	x	x		x	x		x		x		x
PIRA/RIRA	N. Ireland	x	x	x					x		x		
UDA/UFF/UVF	N. Ireland	x	x	x					x		x		
D-Company	Pakistan	x	x	x		x			x		x	x	

73

and grow their infrastructure in the post-Cold War era.[1] One study identifies 12 "watch-points" that constitute the areas where terror-crime collaborations are most likely, including "online gambling, securities fraud, and pirating of intellectual property."[2]

However, most published analyses provide little systematic understanding of how terrorist organizations are, or may be, specifically involved in film piracy. This chapter identifies three ways terrorism and piracy can be linked: a terrorist group may simply adopt or *appropriate*[3] the methods of organized crime; a criminal gang may be induced to move along the continuum from crime toward becoming a terrorist organization; a terrorist group that had used crime to finance its terror may move in the opposite direction once its political objectives are no longer relevant—for example, when an agreement ends most of the differences at issue.

The types of possible linkage might be labeled appropriation, transformation, and transition. Prime candidates for appropriated crimes are ones that do not have steep learning curves, that require minimal up-front investment, and that flourish in areas where state capacity is weak. Transformation could be sudden, triggered by a political or social event, or a slower process in which a group responds to adverse political realities. To be sure, the risks of transformation are high, as groups put at peril their unity based on profit and create enemies opposed to their politics or, more likely, to their use of terrorist tactics against civilians. Transition is likely to be very gradual; it perhaps also reflects the fact that the profits from crime can themselves be corrosive, altering the motivation of terrorist leaders. Groups in transition may maintain a public veneer that masks their underlying profit

---

[1] Angel Rabasa et al., *Beyond al-Qaeda. Part 2: The Outer Rings of the Terrorist Universe*, Santa Monica, CA: RAND Corporation, MG-430-AF, 2006, p. 101.

[2] Louise I. Shelley et al., *Methods and Motives: Exploring Links Between Transnational Organized Crime and International Terrorism*, Washington, D.C.: United States Department of Justice, Document Number 211207, June 23, 2005, p. 14. Available at http://www.ncjrs.gov/pdffiles1/nij/grants/211207.pdf (as of September 12, 2008).

[3] Phil Williams, "Terrorist Financing and Organized Crime: Nexus, Appropriation or Transformation?" in Thomas J. Biersteker and Sue E. Eckert (eds.), *Countering the Financing of Terrorism*, London: Routledge, 2007.

motivations—for instance, they may use their piracy infrastructure to distribute multimedia products that enshrine their political legacy.[4]

The Tri-Border Area (Latin America)[5]

The tri-border area (TBA) of Brazil, Argentina, and Paraguay has been under scrutiny for more than two decades, as it is known to be a haven for a panoply of criminal groups and Islamic terrorist organizations, such as Hezbollah.[6] Smugglers and organized criminals have mingled with terrorists and terrorist financiers of widely disparate ideologies amid one of the world's largest black markets, in the TBA commercial district of Ciudad del Este.[7] The city has become a symbol for the nexus of organized crime and terrorism. Earlier RAND research, along with many experts, identified the TBA as the "most important center for financing Islamic terrorism outside the Middle East."[8] The full case in Appendix B merits reading, as it is the most authoritative account we could compile.

- **Highlight.** This case is built on the strength of actions by the U.S. Treasury Department in 2004 and 2006 to freeze the assets of the Barakat network. To date it is the most in-depth look at Hezbollah's activities in the TBA.
- **Piracy revenue.** The Barakat network is suspected of sending millions of dollars to Hezbollah. Funds were raised from the proceeds of pirated goods and drug trafficking, along with a pervasive protection racket on local Lebanese merchants.

---

[4] Chris Dishman, "Terrorism, Crime, and Transformation," *Studies in Conflict & Terrorism*, Vol. 24, No. 1, 2001, p. 44.

[5] See Appendix B, pp. 48–96, for a more detailed description of this case.

[6] Rex Hudson, *Terrorist and Organized Crime Groups in the Tri-Border Area (TBA) of South America*, Washington, D.C.: Federal Research Division, Library of Congress, July 2003.

[7] Ibid.

[8] Angel Rabasa et al., MG-430-AF, 2006, p. 153.

- **Discovery of piracy.** The Barakat network entered piracy from its very beginnings, and to this day piracy remains central to the network's activities in the TBA.
- **Type of terrorism-piracy link.** In this case, the link was primarily appropriation, as Barakat used piracy and various crimes to raise money for the Hezbollah terrorist organization.
- **Role of law enforcement.** Argentinean intelligence was the first and most active agency monitoring terrorist activity in the TBA. Its efforts, combined with pressure from the U.S. government, prompted Paraguayan courts to prosecute the leaders of the Barakat network for financial crimes.
- **Evidence base.** The evidence for this case is built on court proceedings, reports by international experts on the TBA, and articles from local media. While the local media at times make sensational claims, their basic accuracy is supported by more-reliable sources, such as intelligence dossiers and interviews with trusted local prosecutors.

Years of terrorism investigations by U.S., British, German, and Israeli intelligence agencies culminated in June 2004, when the U.S. Department of the Treasury, Office of Foreign Assets Control (OFAC), named Assad Ahmad Barakat as a "Specially Designated Global Terrorist" for acting as the key financer for Hezbollah in Latin America.[9] OFAC officials froze Barakat's assets and businesses under Executive Order 13224, stating that he used an array of illicit business dealings to generate funding for the Lebanese terrorist organization.[10] "From counterfeiting to extortion," they explained in a press release, "this Hizballah sympathizer committed financial crimes and utilized front companies to underwrite terror."[11] Two years later, OFAC added nine

---

[9] U.S. Department of Treasury, "Treasury Designates Islamic Extremist, Two Companies Supporting Hizballah in Tri-Border Area," press release, June 10, 2004. Available at http://www.treas.gov/press/releases/js1720.htm (as of September 24, 2008).

[10] Ibid.

[11] Ibid.

of Barakat's associates to the terror watch list.[12] The associates are alleged to have continued providing financial and logistical support to Hezbollah while Barakat served out a six-year sentence in Paraguay for tax evasion.[13]

The cases bring a fresh perspective to Barakat and his network of associates in the TBA, demonstrating the link between Barakat's terror financing and a vast piracy operation. The total value of the enterprise is difficult to estimate, but according to intelligence agencies, Barakat provided, and perhaps still provides, a large part of the $20 million sent annually from the TBA to finance Hezbollah.[14] Put into context, this amount is one-third of what Iran contributes[15] and roughly one-fifth of Hezbollah's annual $100 million budget.[16] This account focuses on Barakat and his associates or contacts, but the cultural and social demographics of Ciudad del Este make it an ideal city for the operations of Chinese-speaking criminal groups as well, and some of these, too, have links to Islamic terror.[17]

The TBA has been rife with smuggling and organized-crime activity since it was urbanized by the Stroessner regime in the 1950s as a free-trade zone.[18] By 1994, the TBA economy had peaked at $12 billion in cash transactions, and Ciudad del Este ranked third worldwide behind

---

[12] U.S. Department of Treasury, "Treasury Targets Hizballah Fundraising Network in the Triple Frontier of Argentina, Brazil, and Paraguay," press release, December 6, 2006. Available at http://www.treas.gov/offices/enforcement/ofac/actions/20061206.shtml (as of September 24, 2008).

[13] Ibid.

[14] Matthew Levitt, "Hezbollah Finances: Funding the Party of God," in Giraldo and Trinkunas, 2007.

[15] Blanca Madani, "Hezbollah's Global Finance Network: The Triple Frontier," *Middle East Intelligence Bulletin,* Vol. 4, No. 1, January 2002. Available at http://www.meib.org/articles/0201_l2.htm (as of September 24, 2008).

[16] Foreign Broadcast Information Service, "Investigation reveals money sent from triborder region to Hizballah," FBIS Document ID: LAP20050719000014, trans. from *"ABC Color* [Asunción] in Spanish," July 18, 2005.

[17] Hudson, 2003.

[18] Sebastian Rotella, "Jungle hub for world's outlaws," *Los Angeles Times.* August 24, 1998, p. 1.

Hong Kong and Miami.[19] Roughly 15,000 of the 630,000 residents of Ciudad del Este are of Lebanese origin. Most of them are Muslim and natives of Lebanon's Bekaa Valley, a renowned drug-trafficking hub and the most important locus of Hezbollah's criminal activity.[20] The open sympathies of these Lebanese residents for Hezbollah's cause are predictable and are thus a critical concern for intelligence agencies.

As the full case study details, various agencies have sought to unravel the tangle of terrorist presence in the TBA. Argentinean intelligence suspects that Hezbollah's militant commander and international operative, Imad Fayaz Mugniyah, traveled to the region in 1992 to plan the bombing of the Israeli embassy in Buenos Aires, in which 29 people were killed.[21] Two years later, he returned to direct an attack on the Argentine-Jewish Mutual Association (AMIA), in which 85 people were killed.[22] Mugniyah was named a lead defendant among 22 other conspirators for his role in coordinating the attack.[23] In May 2003, prosecutors issued a warrant for the arrest of Assad Ahmad Barakat, alleging that he had worked with Mugniyah to arrange the trucks and explosives moved through the TBA into Argentina for the AMIA bombing.[24]

Soon thereafter, Khalid Sheikh Mohammed, al Qaeda's "engineer" and the mastermind of the 9/11 attacks, made a trip to the TBA to visit members of the Foz do Iguaçu Muslim community and estab-

---

[19] Ibid.

[20] Angel Rabasa et al., 2006, p. 187.

[21] Foreign Broadcast Information Service, "Argentine prosecutors link tri-border Hizballah leaders to AMIA attack," FBIS Document ID: LAP20030528000104, trans. from *ABC Color* [Asunción], May 28, 2003.

[22] Matthew Levitt and David Schenker, "Who Was Imad Mughniyeh?" *Policywatch #1340*, Washington Institute for Near East Policy, February 14, 2008. Available at http://www.washingtoninstitute.org/templateC05.php?CID=2716 (as of September 28, 2008).

[23] Jeffery Goldberg, "Hezbollah sets up operations in South America and the United States," *New Yorker*, October 28, 2002.

[24] Foreign Broadcast Information Service, "Argentine prosecutors link tri-border Hizballah leaders to AMIA attack," 2003.

lish a charitable entity to finance their terrorist operations.[25] Police data and a visa found in the passport Mohammed carried when he was arrested in 2003 confirm that he was in Brazil for 20 days in December 1995.[26] By various accounts, that trip was the basis for cooperation between Hezbollah and al Qaeda, despite the sharp Shi'a-Sunni sectarian split between the two groups.[27] Argentinean intelligence agencies monitored numerous meetings that suggested continued cooperation and no "operational differences" between Hezbollah and al Qaeda in the TBA.[28] The reliability of Argentina's intelligence has been questioned, however, and to date no active terrorist training camps or military bases have been found in the region.[29]

Assad Ahmad Barakat's network, known locally as the Barakat Clan, is headquartered in Galeria Page, a five-story commercial building in downtown Ciudad del Este.[30] Most of its 165 shops belong to wholesalers who supply goods to thousands of merchants.[31] The mall is also a microcosm of the different forms of crime that flow through the TBA. Examples include counterfeit electronics and pirated goods, unlicensed money exchange and transfer facilities, and illegal cell-phone

---

[25] John C.K. Daly, "The Latin Connection," *Terrorism Monitor*, Vol. 1, Issue 3, October 10, 2003. Available at http://jamestown.org/publications_details.php?volume_id=391&issue_id=2877&article_id=23407 (as of September 28, 2008). "Police: Mohammed visited Brazil in 1995," *CNN International*, March 9, 2003. Available at http://edition.cnn.com/2003/WORLD/americas/03/08/mohammed.brazil/index.html (as of September 24, 2008). Foreign Broadcast Information Service, "Brazilian magazine investigates US-accused terrorist financiers in triborder," FBIS Document ID: LAP20070312357003, trans. from *Epoca* [Rio de Janeiro], March 12, 2007.

[26] Terry McDermott, Josh Meyer, and Patrick J. McDonnell, "The Plots and Designs of Al Qaeda's Engineer," *Los Angeles Times*, March 1, 2003, p. A1.

[27] Ibid.

[28] Mario Daniel Montoya, "War on terrorism reaches Paraguay's triple border," *Jane's Intelligence Review,* December 1, 2001.

[29] A. Brownfeld, "Terrorists in the triple frontier," *Jane's Intelligence Review*, February 12, 2003.

[30] U.S. Department of Treasury, 2006.

[31] Details from U.S. Department of Treasury, 2006; Foreign Broadcast Information Service, "Brazilian magazine investigates US-accused terrorist financiers in triborder," 2007; and Hudson, 2003, p. 26.

cloning stores, as well as fronts for suspected drug running and drug-trafficking operations. The impact of Galeria Page is felt throughout Ciudad del Este, and it continues to be a hub for both licit and illicit activity.

On October 3, 2001, Paraguayan police entered Galeria Page and searched one of Barakat's businesses, Casa Apollo.[32] The evidence they recovered included 60 hours of videotapes of Hezbollah propaganda and CD-ROMS that included instructions for training materials for suicide bombers.[33] A file recovered on Barakat's computer contained Hezbollah military orders for each town and village in southern Lebanon.[34] A paper trail connected Barakat to Sheik Hassan Nasrallah, the Shi'a cleric then at the helm of the militant al Moqawamah (The Resistance) branch of Hezbollah.[35] Police found receipts for money transfers to banks in Lebanon and a letter from Nasrallah to Barakat thanking him for his contributions to a charity called El Matir (The Martyr).[36] El Matir subsidizes families of suicide bombers who have committed their missions of terror.[37]

In November 2003, Barakat was finally delivered to Paraguayan authorities to face charges of tax evasion, unlawful association for crim-

---

[32] Foreign Broadcast Information Service, "Paraguay seeks arrest of Lebanese businessman in Brazil for links to terrorism," FBIS Document ID: LAP20011106000016, trans. from *O Globo* [Rio de Janeiro], November 6, 2001.

[33] Ibid.

[34] U.S. Department of Treasury, 2004.

[35] Foreign Broadcast Information Service, "Nasrallah coordinated funds from tri-border region," FBIS Document ID: LAP20020530000054, trans. from *ABC Color* [Asunción], May 30, 2002.

[36] Ibid.

[37] Foreign Broadcast Information Service, "Evidence shows Hizballah leader transferred funds from Cuidad del Este to ME," FBIS Document ID: LAP20020530000065, trans. from *ABC Color* [Asunción], May 30, 2002.

inal purposes, and advocating the commission of a crime.[38] He was eventually convicted of tax evasion and received a six-year sentence.[39]

Although Barakat had been the biggest Hezbollah target in the region, it was another Lebanese businessman, Ali Khalil Mehri, who was first implicated in a criminal conspiracy involving copyright piracy and terrorism financing from the TBA. His operations were smaller than Barakat's, and by all accounts, he did not have a formal position in the Barakat network.[40] Nonetheless, the two worked in parallel. Mehri housed his operation in the shopping gallery that Barakat dominated.[41] Financial records indicated that Mehri had provided funds to al Moqawamah—the militant branch of Hezbollah with which Barakat is alleged to have worked.

On February 25, 2000, Mehri was taken into custody after Paraguayan anti-terrorist forces used explosive charges to blow in the front door of his Ciudad del Este apartment.[42] The ensuing search of his offices in the Galeria Page and Primavera shopping malls yielded an abundance of counterfeit CDs, video games, and related materials. Prosecutors charged Mehri with intellectual-property violations.[43] He

---

[38] Foreign Broadcast Information Service, "Paraguay: Hizballah Financier Barakat Extradited from Brazil," FBIS Document ID: LAP20031118000030, trans. from Program Summary Excerpt, *Sistema Nacional de Televisión* (SNT TV) [Asunción], November 17, 2003.

[39] Foreign Broadcast Information Service, "Brazilian police arrest Lebanese businessman linked to Iranian government," FBIS Document ID: LAP20060507025001, trans. *ABC Color* [Asunción], May 6, 2006.

[40] None of the major reports cited in this chapter mention any formal connection between Mehri and Barakat. For example, see John L. Lombardi and David J. Sanchez, "Terrorist Financing and the Tri-Border Area of South America: The Challenge of Effective Governmental Response in a Permissive Environment" in Giraldo and Trinkunas, 2007, p. 234.

[41] Foreign Broadcast Information Service, "Evidence shows Hizballah leader transferred funds from Cuidad del Este to ME," 2002.

[42] Foreign Broadcast Information Service, "Paraguayan police arrest Lebanese accused of piracy," 2000.

[43] Foreign Broadcast Information Service, "Report confirms Mehri's piracy activities," FBIS Document ID: LAP20000307000035, trans. from *ABC Color* [Asunción], March 6, 2000.

got out on bail and fled to Brazil, but an associate was convicted of IPR violations and conspiracy and was sentenced to three years in prison.[44]

Mehri made use of a technique employed for years by Chinese organized-crime groups: He took advantage of weak evidentiary requirements and widespread corruption in Paraguay's copyright, trademark, and patent office to obtain certificates that purportedly gave him exclusive rights to manufacture the merchandise that he counterfeited.[45] Mehri's fraudulent certificate for PlayStation, a video game system manufactured legitimately by Sony, is reproduced in Figure 5.1. Pirates and counterfeiters effectively turned Paraguay's intellectual-property system into an extortion mechanism. If merchants tried to sell products that had been "registered," they were subject to extortion, and the police became the ultimate enforcers of this racket.

Thus, one of the dominant modes of terrorist financing in the TBA was enabled by both violating international IPR and at the same time enforcing a corrupt intellectual-property regime in Paraguay. The irony is that pirates in Ciudad del Este understood the economic value of intellectual-property protection just much as the legitimate owners did. Therefore, even in the illicit economy, copyrights, trademarks, and patents, albeit bogus ones, had a place.

Northern Ireland[46]

Historically, the best-documented cases displaying a direct connection between terrorism and counterfeiting involve the Irish Republican Army (IRA). The production and sale of counterfeit products had been a source of revenue for both republican and loyalist paramilitary factions during Northern Ireland's "Troubles" and continued to pro-

---

[44] Foreign Broadcast Information Service, "Higher court upholds jail sentence against Arab's partner," FBIS Document ID: LAP20030721000074, trans. from *Noticias* [Asunción], July 21, 2003.

[45] "Mafia de las marcas (Trademark Mafia)," *ABC Color* [Asunción], May 6, 2004. Available at www.abc.com.py (as of October 1, 2008).

[46] See Appendix B, pp.96–118, for a more detailed description of this case.

Figure 5.1
Mehri's Fraudulent Title for PlayStation

vide a means of financing for splinter groups that persisted after the ceasefire.[47]

Paramilitary groups in Northern Ireland fomented civil unrest and violence for more than 30 years. The conflict is said to have resulted in more than 3,500 deaths in clashes with military forces, as well as terrorist attacks on civilians in both Northern Ireland and the Republic.[48] In 1998, however, the Belfast Agreement began a political process that ended the hostilities and led to the decommissioning of the major terrorist groups. Splinter groups remain, however, and pledge to continue their campaigns; the U.S. government has specified as terrorist organizations the Real IRA, Continuity IRA, the LVF, Orange Volunteers, Red Hand Defenders, and the Ulster Defence Association/Ulster Freedom Fighters (UDA/UFF). With the end of most of the political violence, Northern Ireland has seen a rise in organized crime, including counterfeiting, with former terrorists leveraging their expertise and networks to engage in crime full-time, as the following case demonstrates.

- **Highlight**. This case shows how paramilitary groups used criminal networks of smuggling and racketeering to build a highly profitable counterfeiting industry.
- **Piracy revenues**. It is estimated that loyalist and republican paramilitary groups take in millions of dollars each year through the sale of counterfeit goods. In 2002, police estimated that the Provisional Irish Republican Army (PIRA) made about $1.5 million a year from piracy alone, with the "taxing" on local pirate groups increasing profits even further. This would provide roughly two-thirds of the PIRA's estimated annual running costs.
- **Discovery of piracy**. The paramilitary groups appear to have been active in piracy since the home video market took off in the early 1990s. By the end of the decade, the ease and quality of digital

---

[47] Independent Monitoring Commission of Northern Ireland. Available at http://www.independentmonitoringcommission.org/index.cfm (as of September 24, 2008).

[48] Malcolm Sutton, *Bear in Mind These Dead: An Index of Deaths from the Conflict in Ireland, 1969–1993*, Belfast: Beyond the Pale Publications, 1994.

duplication helped film and software piracy to skyrocket. By 2004, paramilitary groups were estimated to control 80 percent of all film and software piracy in the territory.

- **Type of terrorism-piracy link.** This is a case of transition, as what were, in effect, terrorist groups that engaged in crime to fund their political objectives became criminal groups over time.
- **Role of law enforcement.** The Organized Crime Task Force (OCTF) of the Police Service of Northern Ireland has taken a proactive approach to combating counterfeiting as a means to disrupt paramilitary groups. Increasingly, this has involved working with Irish Customs and Excises to stem the flow of smuggling and counterfeit goods that pass across the border in counties such as South Armagh.
- **Evidence base.** Evidence from this case is built on extensive interviews with the OCTF. In addition, a report by the British House of Commons Northern Ireland Affairs Select Committee provides a clear case for the paramilitary activity in organized crime and highlights the money to be made from piracy.

As stated in 2002 by Jane Kennedy, Minister of State for Northern Ireland, "One destructive legacy of the Troubles is that the terrorist godfathers have been able to use the organisational networks that are in place, combined with the fear that they engender within their communities, to line their own pockets, for whatever purpose. Keeping control of the communities in order to make money has become an end in itself."[49]

The issue came to the forefront in a report on the financing of terrorism issued by British House of Commons Northern Ireland Affairs Select Committee in 2002. Members sounded the alarm that terrorist fundraising in Northern Ireland was increasingly turning "to more complex and sophisticated forms of organised criminal activity such as

---

[49] United Kingdom House of Commons, *The Financing of Terrorism in Northern Ireland: Interim Report on the Proceeds of Crime Bill, HC 628*, Northern Ireland Affairs, Fourth Report, n.d. Available at http://www.publications.parliament.uk/pa/cm200102/cmselect/cmniaf/978/97803.htm#a1 (as of September 23, 2008).

fuel smuggling and counterfeiting."[50] When the Independent Monitoring Committee was established in 2004 to oversee the implementation of the Belfast Accords, it drew similar conclusions. In its view, the seriousness of the threat posed by paramilitary groups engaging in robbery, extortion, smuggling, and counterfeiting was "the biggest long-term threat to the rule of law in Northern Ireland."[51] The trend continued in the ensuing years and reached a high-water mark in late 2004, when the OCTF estimated that paramilitary groups were involved in "80 percent of all counterfeiting and piracy" in the territory.[52]

The case study summarized below demonstrates how the remaining dissident members, stripped of their ideological struggles, had their long-standing criminal underpinnings exposed. In sum, it shows what many analysts of the Northern Ireland conflict have known for some time—that for some leaders of the republican and loyalist groups, material gain was equally, if not more, important than the political cause.

Since the 1970s, the porous border between the Republic and Northern Ireland has provided smugglers with dozens of routes to move goods to arm and finance both sides of the terrorist campaigns. In addition to a steady flow of arms and munitions, paramilitaries smuggled livestock grain, cattle and pigs, stolen cars, petroleum, cigarettes, and lighters.[53] Having avoided paying proper value-added tax (VAT) or customs duties, the paramilitaries sold contraband items, especially cigarettes and fuel, at steep discounts. As late as 2005, authorities estimated that one-third of all cigarettes in Northern Ireland were smuggled, and

---

[50] Ibid.

[51] Independent Monitoring Commission of Northern Ireland, *First Report of the Independent Monitoring Commission*, April 2004, paragraph 6.13. Available at http://www.independent-monitoringcommission.org/documents/uploads/First%20Report.doc (as of September 24, 2008).

[52] Organized Crime Task Force, Police Service of Northern Ireland, "New Research on Counterfeiting Looks Towards Consumers," press release, September 28, 2004. Available at http://www.octf.gov.uk/index.cfm/section/News/page/details/key/D03F3464-B0D0-7815-0FEA6E167DAEBD29/?month=9&year=2004 (as of September 28, 2008).

[53] John Horgan and Max Taylor, "Playing the 'Green Card'—Financing the Provisional IRA: Part 1," *Terrorism and Political Violence*, Vol. 11, No. 2, Summer 1999, pp. 1–38.

half of the territory's filling stations sold smuggled fuel, causing the government to lose more than $400 million in revenue each year.[54]

Counterfeiting, with its high profit margins, provided an attractive business opportunity that fit neatly with other illicit enterprises. The paramilitary piracy industry appears to have been around since the home video and personal computer markets took off in the late 1980s. The paramilitary groups were primarily interested in the manufacture and wholesaling of such goods, which is "where the profitability lies."[55] The sale of pirated films, music, and computer games continued to grow over the decade, and the sourcing of master copies might well have been enhanced by strong republican ties to the United States.[56] The trade proliferated on both sides when the ease of digital duplication arrived and as Internet piracy made masters of films and software more readily available. Seizures of pirate products from all groups reached a total of £3.5 million yearly at the turn of the century.[57]

The estimates are slippery, but in addition to the PIRA's take from piracy, which was noted earlier, other groups' operating costs and fundraising capacities are summarized in Table 5.2.[58] The data in the table demonstrate just how able the groups were to raise funds to meet their budget needs. Furthermore, while the groups had relatively lean operating costs, the costs to governments to counter the paramilitary groups were exponentially higher. Experts have calculated that for every £1 raised by paramilitaries and spent in the terrorist campaign,

---

[54] David Lister and Sean O'Neill, "IRA plc turns from terror into biggest crime gang in Europe," *The Times*, February 25, 2005. Available at http://www.timesonline.co.uk/article/0,,2-1499253,00.html (as of September 28, 2008).

[55] United Kingdom House of Commons, n.d.

[56] Lister and O'Neill, 2005.

[57] Memorandum submitted by the Police Service of Northern Ireland to the United Kingdom House of Commons Northern Ireland Affairs Select Committee, n.d. Available at http://www.publications.parliament.uk/pa/cm200102/cmselect/cmniaf/978/2011602.htm (as of September 24, 2008).

[58] Richard Evans, "Organised crime and terrorist financing in Northern Ireland," *Jane's Intelligence Review*, August 9, 2002.

Table 5.2
Running Costs vs. Fundraising Capacity of Northern Ireland Paramilitary Groups

Organization[a]	Estimated running costs (per year)	Estimated fundraising capacity (per year)
Provisional IRA(PIRA)	£1.5m	£5–8 million
Real IRA(RIRA)	£500,00	£5 million
Continuity IRA(CIRA)	£25,000–30,000	
INLA	£25,000–30,000	£500,000
UDA	£500,000	£500,000–1 million
UFF	£250,000	
UVF	£1–2million	£1.5 million
LVF	£50,000	£2 million

SOURCE: Police Service of Northern Ireland estimates, 2003.
[a]Each of the organizations might use several means of financing, including fuel, tobacco, and alcohol smuggling; drugs; counterfeit goods; armed robberies; extortion; and membership subscription. In some cases, the brigades themselves are expected to be self-financing (United Kingdom House of Commons, "The Financing of Terrorism in Northern Ireland," n.d.).

the governments of Britain and the Republic of Ireland spent an average of £130 on countering and repairing terrorist damage.[59]

Once the digital revolution hit, republican and loyalist groups used the same infrastructure to burn movies and to duplicate propaganda videos intended to advance their ideological causes and recruit new members. The contents of these videos ranged from demonstrations of force to rallying cries from leaders. The libraries were extensive and known to be an active part of cultivating the fear these groups sought to project and the respect they sought. In a raid in Jonesborough, described below, authorities found a propaganda collection of six volumes alongside pirated Hollywood films and pornography.[60]

---

[59] Andrew Silke, "In Defense of the Realm: Financing Loyalist Terrorism in Northern Ireland: Part One: Extortion and Blackmail," *Studies in Conflict & Terrorism*, Vol. 21, No. 4, 1998, pp. 331–333.

[60] Primary document: Photograph of Jonesborough Raids, received from Police Service of Northern Ireland, September 28, 2006.

Despite significant progress made by law enforcement in decommissioning terrorist groups and policing organized crime, paramilitary involvement in piracy continued. In its 2007 Annual Report and Threat Assessment, the OCTF and Independent Monitoring Commission confirmed that major paramilitary organizations on both sides were still linked to organized-crime activity.[61] In that report, the Ulster Defence Association (UDA), Ulster Volunteer Force (UVF), and PIRA were singled out as active in counterfeiting and having varying involvement in extortion, drug dealing, and other financial crimes.

It should be noted, however, that the leadership of all of these organizations had attempted to persuade their members away from crime. The PIRA leadership specifically instructed its members in 2005 not to engage in criminal activity.[62] But although crime is no longer sanctioned by the paramilitary organizations, the low-risk/high-profit model of counterfeiting remains appealing and evidently ingrained into the shadow economies of Northern Ireland. According to the annual statistics, the OCTF seized over £3 million in counterfeit goods in 2007. In this haul, the piracy of films remained the most profitable category—the total street value of the pirated films seized was an estimated £997,095.[63]

One specific case makes piracy by Northern Ireland's paramilitary splinter groups more vivid. On December 13, 2000, three Irish Customs and Excises officers searched a suspected fuel-laundering plant in Carrickaneena, just feet from the border between the Republic and Northern Ireland.[64] A significant difference in diesel taxation between the two countries created a potentially lucrative black market, of which

---

[61] Independent Monitoring Commission of Northern Ireland, *Seventeenth Report of the Independent Monitoring Commission*, November 2007, paragraphs 2.15 and 2.16. Available at http://www.independentmonitoringcommission.org/documents/uploads/17th_IMC.pdf (as of September 24, 2008).

[62] Ibid.

[63] Police Service of Northern Ireland, *Organized Crime Task Force Annual Report and Threat Assessment*, 2007. Available at http://www.octf.gov.uk (as of September 20, 2008).

[64] Tom Brady and Elaine Keogh, "Real IRA hold up Gardai to steal back seized haul," *The Irish Independent*, December 14, 2000. While the documentation of this account is only media reporting, Joathan Dotan's interviews with police authorities provide confirmation.

authorities maintained that the PIRA had taken full advantage. Red diesel, a rebated fuel designated for limited-use vehicles, is sometimes "laundered" by chemically removing the dye so that the fuel can be sold at a higher price. During the search, the Customs and Excises officers discovered a van full of what appeared to be counterfeit DVDs, CDs, and videogames. They summoned the Gardai (the police force of the Republic of Ireland), which has jurisdiction in cases of alleged counterfeiting.[65]

The Gardai found that the van contained some £100,000 worth of pirated films, CDs, and videogames,[66] as well as DVD burners.[67] Moreover, a mobile stall attached to the van had been seen selling product in the Jonesborough Market.[68] After finishing the seizure, the Gardai were preparing to head back to their station when a pair of rockets were fired skyward from an area reportedly on the Northern Ireland side of the border.[69] Seconds later, vehicles pulled up, and seven men emerged wearing camouflage clothing and ski masks, wielding firearms and iron bars.[70] The seven men held the three unarmed officers at gunpoint and demanded that the Gardai return the stall, the van, and its contents.[71] The officers did not put up any resistance, and the men barricaded them in a shed and escaped with the goods. The men then proceeded to drive the van from the location north toward Jonesborough.[72] The officers did not give chase.[73]

The Gardai later told the media that they were "convinced" the perpetrators were members of the Real Irish Republican Army (RIRA),

---

[65] Ibid.

[66] Elaine Keogh, "'Real IRA' believed to be behind hold up of Gardai," *Irish Times*, December 14, 2000.

[67] Brady and Keogh, 2000.

[68] Ibid.

[69] Paddy Clancy, "Real IRA swoop on cops," *The Sun*, December 14, 2000.

[70] Keogh, 2000.

[71] Clancy, 2000.

[72] Keogh, 2000.

[73] Ibid.

a radical arm of the PIRA.[74] Incidentally, the ambush coincided with the run-up to Christmas intended to, as Gardai sources told the press, "raise funds for the Real IRA."[75] The ambush was also executed less than 24 hours after U.S. President Bill Clinton visited neighboring Dundalk to make an appeal for a permanent peace in Northern Ireland.[76]

South Asia[77]

The case of Dawood Ibrahim, India's godfather of criminal gangs from Bangkok to Dubai, demonstrates the blurring line between crime and terror around the globe. In his early years, Ibrahim's gang, D-Company, pursued the standard crime-syndicate practices of extortion, smuggling, and contract killings.[78] Since the 1980s, however, Ibrahim and his cohorts have been able to vertically integrate D-company throughout the Indian film and pirate industry, forging a clear pirate monopoly over competitors and launching a racket to control the master copies of pirated Bollywood and Hollywood films.

In 1993, D-Company was transformed into a terrorist organization when it carried out the "Black Friday" Mumbai bombings, an attack that killed more than 257 people and injured an estimated 713.[79] Later, D-Company developed ties to al Qaeda and the Kashmiri terrorist group, Lakshar-e-Taiyiba (LeT) while its leaders were exiled in Pakistan.[80] For all these reasons, in 2003, the U.S. Treasury Department Office of Foreign Assets Control (OFAC) added Ibrahim to its

---

[74] Clancy, 2000.

[75] Ibid.

[76] Brady and Keogh, 2000.

[77] See Appendix B, pp. 118–140, for a more detailed description of this case.

[78] S. Hussain Zaidi, *Black Friday: The True Story of the Bombay Bomb Blasts*, New Delhi and New York: Penguin Books, 2002, p. 25.

[79] Anil Singh, "Temkar Street and Two Terrorists," *Times of India,* October 7, 2006.

[80] James Robbins, "The Mumbai Blasts," *National Review Online,* July 12, 2006. Available at http://article.nationalreview.com/?q=MDc5MGNjYmEyYWQ1MmE1Y2NiYzY5ZTBhZ mNmZDZmNmU= (as of October 1, 2008).

terrorist watch list and froze his assets.[81] Shortly thereafter, the United Nations Security Council's al Qaeda and Taliban Sanctions Committee issued a similar order.[82]

- **Highlight.** This case demonstrates how an existing organized crime group that turned into a terrorist group leveraged rackets in the film industry to vertically expand into piracy.
- **Piracy revenues.** While there are no estimates of D-Company's proceeds from film piracy, the size and sophistication of Ibrahim's counterfeit DVD operation bespeak a highly profitable enterprise.
- **Discovery of piracy.** D-Company was readily able to transition to film piracy through its well-established influence in the Bollywood movie industry. The syndicate's Al-Mansoor and SADAF brands acquired extraordinary market power in the distribution of pirated films throughout the region.
- **Type of terrorism-piracy link.** While the Northern Ireland terrorist groups aged into pure criminality, this case illustrates the crossing of the line in the opposite direction, as D-Company transformed into an organization not just passively supporting terrorists, but with close links to them.
- **Role of law enforcement.** Indian authorities had been aware of D-Company's film piracy operations in Pakistan since the 1990s but were practically powerless to intervene. Only after 2005, when U.S. Customs seized a large shipment of SADAF-brand counterfeit discs in Virginia, did Pakistani authorities, under a threat of trade sanctions, begin raiding D-Company's duplicating facilities in Karachi.

---

[81] "U.S. Designates Dawood Ibrahim as Terrorist Supporter," Washington, D.C.: Office of Public Affairs, United States Department of Treasury, October 16, 2003. Available at http://www.treas.gov/press/releases/js909.htm (as of September 24, 2008).

[82] United Nations Security Council, *Security Council Al-Qaida, Taliban Sanctions Committee Approves Changes to Consolidated List*, Department of Public Information, July 25, 2006. Available at http://www.un.org/News/Press/docs/2006/sc8785.doc.htm (as of September 24, 2008).

- **Evidence base.** Much of this case is based on secondary and media sources, although authorities have long been aware of many of D-Company's operations. The U.S. designation of Ibrahim as a terrorist provided and confirmed details about Ibrahim's transformation into terror.

Ibrahim systematically recruited gangsters from all neighborhoods of Mumbai and built them into the city's dominant criminal syndicate, the D-Company, which focused on three areas: smuggling goods (gold, silver, electronic products, and textiles), extorting protection money from local business industries (hotels, construction, iron, steel, grain, textiles, and diamond merchants), and vice (gambling and prostitution).[83] By the end of the 1980s, Ibrahim was the undisputed underworld "kingpin" of Mumbai.[84]

In 1992, India's trade liberalization policies changed the economics of the gold and silver market and made smuggling less lucrative.[85] To make up for the losses, Ibrahim sought to diversify his business lines, first taking on narcotics and arms trafficking, then moving his racketeering into the entertainment business. This afforded Ibrahim the double benefit of raising his social status and also enabling him to serve as a loan shark for dozens of producers who desperately needed his funds. Furthermore, D-Company's power increased dramatically as it began to control more facets of the film production process, culminating with piracy.[86]

Over a decade and a half, D-Company vertically integrated into every part of the Indian filmmaking industry. It began with loan-sharking in film production, then progressed into film distribution,

---

[83] Zaidi, 2002, p. 25.

[84] "Profile of Dawood Ibrahim (2001)," South Asia Terrorism Portal. Available at http://satp.org/ (as of April 1, 2008).

[85] Sumita Sarkar and Arvind Tiwari, "Combating Organised Crime: A Case Study of Mumbai City," *Faultlines,* Vol. 12, 2002. Available at http://www.satp.org/satporgtp/publication/faultlines/volume12/Article5.htm (as of September 24, 2008).

[86] "India's Fugitive Gangster," *BBC News*, September 12, 2006. Available at http://news.bbc.co.uk/2/hi/south_asia/4775531.stm (as of October 1, 2008).

home-video manufacturing, and—a natural culmination of its rackets—film piracy. Amid the challenges D-Company endured in this critical period, from 1990 to the late 2000s, film enterprises withstood the test of time as a reliable illicit-revenue stream.

Although India's prolific film industry had been a profit center and cultural icon for decades, it was, surprisingly, not recognized by the government as a legitimate industry until 1998.[87] This status barred legitimate financial institutions and private investors from financing films. Ibrahim tasked his brother Noora with stepping into this vacuum and providing debt financing to major Indian filmmakers.[88] The terms assigned to these loans were clearly exploitative.

The next step was moving into distribution. As the Indian diaspora grew, distribution rights became increasingly valuable: Ready audiences developed in the United States, the United Kingdom, and the Gulf States. D-company's seat of power in Dubai allowed it to aggressively seek and control distribution rights for the Gulf countries and Pakistan.[89] Customs data reveal that the company had a booming export business in Karachi, Pakistan,[90] and for good reason: All Indian films distributed in Pakistan were pirated, and therefore more profitable, because importing Indian films was illegal.[91]

In the process, D-Company gained control of the SADAF Trading Company based in Karachi, which allowed the gang to better organize distribution in Pakistan and, more important, acquire the infrastructure to manufacture pirate VHS tapes and VCDs for sale all over

---

[87] Monika Mehta, "Globalizing Bombay Cinema," *Cultural Dynamics*, Vol. 17, No. 2, 2005, pp. 135–154.

[88] Sarkar and Tiwari, 2002.

[89] Gilbert King, *The Most Dangerous Man in the World: Dawood Ibrahim: Billionaire Gangster, Protector of Osama Bin Laden, Nuclear Black Market Entrepreneur, Islamic Extremist, and Global Terrorist*, New York: Chamberlain Bros., 2004.

[90] International Federation of the Phonographic Industry, Pakistan, customs records showing multiple shipments of product from Karachi to Al Mansoor as late as 2003.

[91] "Pakistan to Show Bollywood Film," *BBC News*, January 23, 2006. Available at http://news.bbc.co.uk/2/hi/entertainment/4639216.stm (as of October 1, 2008).

the world.[92] Still, SADAF's biggest exports were to India, which, due to lax anti-piracy enforcement on the part of Indian authorities, remained an open channel. Bollywood and Hollywood products duplicated at SADAF's plant were readily smuggled into the country via Nepal.[93]

Once D-Company's control of the production, distribution, and manufacturing/piracy operations was in place, the gang was able to launch a racket to control the masters of most Bollywood and dubbed Hollywood films distributed in India.[94] This powerful vertical integration provided D-Company a clear monopoly over other competitors. And with various methods of control—including the killing of renegade pirates—D-Company had the wherewithal to demand that pirates obey their terms and timelines of release, or else face retaliation.[95] From start to finish, D-Company dominated every step of the Indian filmmaking process and so was able to control most of the region's piracy.

The Bottom Line

Although three cases hardly support definitive conclusions, they do illustrate several forms of convergence between organized crime, piracy, and terrorism. In all of them, the terrorists' link to piracy was sustained for years. The cases show how resilient piracy can be, not only to changing market conditions, but also to internal operational changes. In terms of the three types of connections, the terrorist financiers in the TBA used a variety of methods employed by organized-crime groups without having to merge with them. Piracy and extortion are easier to appropriate than narcotics trafficking. In the end, whether the TBA case is one of appropriation or transformation turns on interpretations of Barakat and Mehri: Were they criminals who sympathized with and supported Hezbollah, or were they Hezbollah operatives running crim-

---

[92] Nishant Bhuse, "D and C Gangs in Rs 100 Cr Piracy," *Mid Day*, June 25, 2005.

[93] Nishant Bhuse, "Pak Piracy Firm Offers Rs 1 Cr for Rdb," *Mid Day*, January 30, 2006.

[94] This rests on multiple examples of evidence. See Appendix B, pp. XXX-xxx.

[95] Bhuse, 2006.

inal operations to support the organization? The answer turns, perhaps, on the unknowable: Did they think they worked for themselves or for Hezbollah?

The case of D-Company's transformation from a criminal to a terrorist organization demonstrates the attendant risks and advantages of this type of linkage. After the Mumbai bombings in 1993, D-Company suffered from defections from its ranks, internal rivalries, and restricted movement for its leadership.[96] At the same time, Ibrahim's terrorist credentials helped win the patronage of the Pakistani intelligence services.[97] What is striking about this case is how quickly D-Company transformed. In a matter of weeks, Ibrahim's top leadership took on an extremist mindset to execute the group's first terrorist attack.[98] In the end, however, the group's relationship with its original terrorist sponsor, Pakistani intelligence, became parasitical, and it may have been forced deeper into terrorism than its leadership had wanted.[99]

Both republican and loyalist groups in Northern Ireland made the transition from terrorism to the enterprise of full-time crime. The "commercialization" of these groups began years before the hostilities stopped, but both were able to use their piracy infrastructure to maintain some sort of political legacy.[100] In the cases presented in this report, piracy dovetailed with extortion, providing the pirates protected spaces in which to manufacture and sell their merchandise with little competition. This required that certain paramilitary structures of each of the organizations remain intact. Thus, one implication of the transition type of connection between terror and crime is that terrorist groups might well be able to reorganize quickly and perhaps regain power because they retain control of territory.

---

[96] King, 2004.

[97] John Wilson, *Karachi, a Terror Capital in the Making*, New Delhi: Rupa & Co., in association with Observer Research Foundation, 2003, p. 29.

[98] Marika Vicziany, "Understanding the 1993 Mumbai Bombings: Madrassas and the Hierarchy of Terror," *South Asia: Journal of South Asian Studies,* Vol. 30, No. 1, April 2007, pp. 43–73.

[99] S. Balakrishnan, "Dawood Clips Anees, Shakeel's Wings," *Times of India,* February 10, 2007.

[100] Horgan and Taylor, 1999, pp. 1–38.

CHAPTER SIX

The Role of Governments: "Protected Spaces" for Crime

The degree of interaction between governments and organized criminal syndicates and possibly terrorist groups is often unclear, as is the degree of tolerance shown by the former toward the activities of the latter. This chapter explores some of these connections. In the Russian case, as organized crime sought to move toward legitimate business, it built on preexisting connections to officials at all levels—cultivating senior officials, bribing others, and intimidating still others—though the criminal activities and violence continued. In the Mexican case, the stakes of politicians led them to tolerate, or even create, "protected spaces" for criminal activity. In Japan, protected spaces for crime continued despite a police crackdown, and the *yakuza*, a masterless criminal class bound by a tradition of honor and duty, sustained a very visible public presence; an afterglow of corruption remained from decades in which the *yakuza* and police were tacit allies.

Russia[1]

In the words of one commentator, Russian organized crime has "adapted" to the changes that have occurred in Russia since the fall of the Soviet Union by developing "a complex relationship with the

---

[1] See Appendix C, pp. 141–165, for a more detailed description of this case.

private market."[2] In so doing, criminal groups have tried to become more businesslike by funneling their illegal profits into legitimate businesses.[3] For Russian organized crime, it is more about business than about violence. As another commentator observed: "Today's criminal wears an Armani suit instead of a leather jacket, and his best friend is his accountant, not his bodyguard."[4] "To put it crudely, once the bank-robber owns the bank, he tends to discourage bank-robbery as a profession."[5]

While it is certainly true that the widespread chaos of the 1990s, which saw violent turf wars between criminal groups in Moscow, St. Petersburg, Yekaterinburg, and Vladivostok[6] and bankers regularly targeted for kidnapping or assault,[7] is a thing of the past, it is equally true that the corruption and use of force has hardly diminished. Instead, Russian organized crime has settled into a pattern closer to that of the 1970s and 1980s, in which corruption of politicians and police is used to eliminate outside interference.[8]

When Russia began privatizing state assets in 1992, organized crime was able to insert itself further into the market by buying up firms with its profits from the Soviet period.[9] Some commentators believe that this involvement in legitimate business has gradually pacified organized crime, highlighting comments that criminals are putting

---

[2] Vsevolod Sokolov, "From Guns to Briefcases: The Evolution of Russian Organized Crime," *World Policy Journal*, Vol. 21, Spring 2004, p. 68.

[3] Ibid.

[4] Ibid., p. 72.

[5] "Mafiya: Organized Crime in Russia," *Janes Intelligence Review—Special Report*, June 1996.

[6] Tom Hunter, "Russia's mafiyas: The new revolution," *Jane's Intelligence Review*, June 1997.

[7] "Mafiya: Organized Crime in Russia," 1996.

[8] Sokolov, 2004, p. 68.

[9] James O. Finckenauer and Yuri A. Voronin, *The Threat of Russian Organized Crime*, Washington, D.C.: National Institute of Justice, June 2001, p. 12. Available at http://www.ncjrs.gov/pdffiles1/nij/187085.pdf (as of September 24, 2008).

their violent pasts behind them, working with government officials,[10] and trying to nurture their businesses.[11]

Nevertheless, organized crime is involved in a wide variety of illegal activities other than providing protection. Criminal groups involved in film piracy have bought into legitimate businesses; however, the purpose has been criminal as well as commercial, creating access to markets to sell the pirated goods as well as facilities to manufacture them. The groups have continued to use violence to keep control of their businesses and to eliminate outsiders who may threaten them. They also continue to take advantage of Russia's ranking of 143 out of 179 on Transparency International's *2007 Corruption Perceptions Index*.[12] Widespread bribery and collusion with police and lawmakers have enabled piracy to continue largely uninterrupted, as is suggested by the following cases.

Russia's widespread corruption, particularly within its law enforcement organizations, provides numerous opportunities for pirates to create protected spaces. For instance, the officers from the economic-crimes squad are known to shut a business down without cause only to require payment in order to restart the business.[13] The going rate is believed to be about $30,000 to get an advance warning of an upcoming raid of a pirate plant, more if it is a large plant,[14] and pirate syndicates have been permitted by corrupt officials to operate on government property and even from prison.[15] In 2005 alone, 4,269 Russian

---

[10] Sokolov, 2004, p. 72.

[11] Sokolov, 2004, p. 70.

[12] *2007 Corruption Perceptions Index*, Transparency International. Available at http://www.transparency.org/policy_research/surveys_indices/cpi/2007 (as of September 29, 2008).

[13] Marielle Eudes, "Russian business feels the heat of corrupt police," *Agence France-Presse*, January 25, 2002.

[14] Jonathan Dotan, interviews with the Russian Anti-Piracy Organization (RAPO) and Russian Phonographic Association (RPA), Moscow, October 4–13, 2006.

[15] Foreign Broadcast Information Service, "Russian hacker magazine reports 2004 piracy figures," FBIS Document ID: CEP20050727030001, trans. from *Khaker*, June 1, 2005; Sabrina Tavernise, "Moscow Journal; Russian Music Pirates Sail on Government Land," *The New York Times*, August 20, 2002. Available at http://query.nytimes.com/gst/fullpage.html?res=9900E4DB113DF933A1575BC0A9649C8B63 (as of October 1, 2008)..

police officers were charged with corruption-related crimes.[16] At one point, Moscow's GUVD (main Internal Affairs Directorate) was considered "gangs of werewolves in police uniforms."[17] Police corruption has become so serious that Russia's Prosecutor General, Alexander Ustinov, declared, "Crime is getting bolder and bolder, and is increasingly penetrating into state law enforcement bodies . . . .. Recent events testify to the fact that organized crime has gained a strong foothold in customs checkpoints, feeling quite comfortable there."[18] Even Russian President Vladimir Putin acknowledged in 2004 that "the state as a whole and the law enforcement bodies, unfortunately, are still afflicted with corruption and inefficiency."[19]

Raiding Victoria, Gamma, and Russobit-Soft

Owners of pirate DVD factories in Russia have been especially eager to take advantage of law enforcement corruption. On March 10 and 11, 2007, police raided the Victoria optical-disc plant in St. Petersburg and seized eight DVD lines capable of pressing 800,000 DVDs per month, five molds, and 258 DVD stampers containing a variety of Hollywood titles.[20] Although the plant was sealed and put under surveillance,[21] police learned that it was making DVDs again because its license had yet to be revoked.[22] A second raid was launched in August 2007 which resulted in the seizure of 55,000 DVDs and illegal molds.[23]

---

[16] "Russian police crime rate up—Interior Ministry," *BBC Monitoring International Reports*, January 31, 2006.

[17] Sokolov, 2004, p. 71.

[18] Foreign Broadcast Information Service, "Russia: Prosecutor Says Organized Crime National Threat," FBIS Document ID: CEP20060515027065, trans. from *ITAR-TASS* [Moscow], May 15, 2006.

[19] Steven Lee Myers, "Pervasive corruption in Russia is 'just called business,'" *The New York Times*, August 13, 2005. Available at http://www.indem.ru/en/Publicat/Pervasive.htm

[20] MPA internal report, March 15, 2007. Also see Nick Holdsworth, "Russian Anti-Piracy Efforts Drive DVD Sales," *The Hollywood Reporter*, March 20, 2007. Available at http://www.allbusiness.com/services/motion-pictures/4778555-1.html (as of October 1, 2008).

[21] Ibid.

[22] MPA internal report, September 28, 2007.

[23] Ibid.

- **Highlight.** These cases demonstrate the symbiosis of Russian pirates and enforcement officials prepared to be on the take.
- **Piracy revenue.** Piracy revenue was a primary part of these operations, on a very large scale.
- **Discovery of piracy.** The factories had long been suspected, or known, to be producers of pirated DVDs.
- **Role of law enforcement.** Enforcement was split, with some authorities on the take, while others were prepared to raid from time to time. Most raids, however, were tipped in advance to the operators of the factories.
- **Evidence base.** The evidence base consists mostly of translations of newspaper articles, corroborated where possible with on-site reports by industry officials.

The Gamma plant, which shares a warehouse with the Victoria plant and is controlled by the same people, was first raided at the end of February 2007.[24] Gamma had the capacity to press 100 million DVDs a year, making it the largest factory ever found in Russia.[25] The plant was raided again on September 24, 2007, after Moscow-based police discovered it had begun making pirate DVDs again under the protection of local police. However, security at the plant gave the operators a chance to destroy some of the evidence.[26]

The Russobit-Soft factory also used corrupt authorities to further its pirate activity. Founded by Oleg Gordiyko[27] in 1998, the company is Russia's largest manufacturer of optical discs,[28] producing more than 2 million discs a month.[29] Dmitry Korovin, a journalist, charged in a

---

[24] MPA internal report, March 15, 2007.

[25] MPA internal reports, March 7 and 15, 2007.

[26] MPA internal report, September 28, 2007.

[27] Foreign Broadcast Information Service, "Selection List: MMU Russian Press," FBIS Document ID: CEP20040817000124, trans. from *Kommersant* [Moscow], August 17, 2004.

[28] "About the Russobit-Soft Company" ("О Компании Руссобит-Софт"). Available at http://translate.google.com/translate?hl=en&sl=ru&u=http://www.russobit-m.ru/&sa=X&oi=translate&resnum=1&ct=result&prev=/search%3Fq%3Drussobit%26hl%3Den%26sa%3DG (as of October 1, 2008).

[29] "Russian Plant in CD Piracy Suits," *FT Investor* (*Pulses*), December 19, 2003.

November 2002 magazine article[30] that Russobit-Soft's managers used their positions on the intellectual-property committee of the Russian Chamber of Commerce, a committee Gordiyko heads,[31] to force out other pirates so that Russobit-Soft could control the market.[32] Gordiyko and the company sued Korovin for libel, but a judgment was returned in Korovin's favor, providing indirect confirmation of his story.[33]

Tarantsev

Alexander Tarantsev, who was linked to organized crime by Russian organized-crime authorities, controlled pirate markets throughout Moscow, including Mitinsky, Danilovsky, Dorgomilovsky, Pokrovsky, and Tuszynsky.[34] He also used bribery to influence government authorities.

- **Highlight.** This case highlights the continuing links between pirates and authorities, not only through bribery but also through the careful cultivation of senior politicians and officials. It is also noteworthy for highlighting the continuing violence.
- **Piracy revenue.** Piracy revenue was a significant part of these operations, as Tarantsev sought to be a presence in the large marketplaces.

---

[30] Alexander Shashkov, "Russian court delays verdict on reporter accused of libel," FBIS Document ID: CEP20040401000032, trans. from *ITAR-TASS* [Moscow], April 1, 2004.

[31] Foreign Broadcast Information Service, "Selection List: MMU Russian Press," FBIS Document ID: CEP20040817000124, trans. from *Kommersant* [Moscow], August 17, 2004.

[32] "Moscow court clears journalist of libel charges," *RIA Novosti*, August 17, 2004.

[33] Foreign Broadcast Information Service, "Selection List: MMU Russian Press," 2004.

[34] "To whom do the Moscow Markets belong? Telman Ismailov, Zarah Iliev, Alexander Tarantsev, Orehovskie, Medvedkovskie, Tolyattinskie and other authoritarian entrepreneurs" ("Кому принадлежат московские рынки. Тельман Исмаилов, Зарах Илиев, Александр Таранцев, Ореховские, Медведковские, Тольяттинские И Другие Авторитетные Предприниматели"), *Sekretinfo* (Секретинфо), September 9, 2003. Available at http://www.informacia.ru/2006/news11062.htm. "Oligarchs" of the criminal world" ("Олигархи Криминального Мира"). Available at http://www.mokryxa.narod.ru/mokryxa/olig.html. "Russian Gold." Available at http://www.opticgifts.info/russian-gold.html (as of October 1, 2008).

- **Discovery of piracy.** The markets had long been beehives of illegal commerce, including various forms of counterfeiting. For that reason, they were attractive to Tarantsev.
- **Role of law enforcement.** The cases continue, as law enforcement has been bought, intimidated, or eliminated.
- **Evidence base.** Since there has been no trial in ten years, the evidence base consists mostly of translations of newspaper articles, corroborated where possible by on-site reports of industry officials, along with some documents.

In November 1997, Alexander Tarantsev was arrested in Miami for falsifying his visa application by failing to acknowledge two previous convictions.[35] After his arrest, the Russian Regional Directorate for Combating Organized Crime (RUOP) began publicly declaring him in league with organized crime,[36] even providing Russian media with confiscated videos showing Tarantsev's lavish lifestyle and shared evidence it had collected with U.S. law enforcement.[37] However, the U.S. judge hearing the case refused to consider the Russian evidence, and the charges eventually were dropped.[38]

In pursuit of influence, Tarantsev had given equipment to various police units in the Moscow area and had donated almost $2 million to a fund he created to help veteran and wounded employees in

---

[35] Personal Profile: Alexander Tarantsev" ("Личное дело: Таранцев Александр Петрович"), *Kommersant*, January 18, 2008. Available at http://www.kommersant.ru/doc.aspx?DocsID=843186. Igor Korotchenko, "Of what it is accused Tarantsev?" Available at http://www.opticgifts.info/of-at-it-is-aused-tarantsev.html (as of October 1, 2008).

[36] Korotchenko, n.d.; "Russian Gold," n.d.; Larisa Kislinkskaya, "Blood on the 'Russian Gold," ("Кровь На Русском Золоте"), *Top Secret* (Совершенно Секретно), October 2007. Available at http://www.compromat.ru/main/mafiamsk/orehovskietarantsev1.htm (as of October 1, 2008).

[37] Vitaly Romanov, "'Russia Gold' does not want to pass for 'Russian Mafia,'" *Segodnya*, Russian Press Digest, December 2, 1997; Korotchenko, n.d.

[38] Sergei Bobylev, "Alexander Tarantsev – A man who makes gold" ("Александр Таранцев – человек, который делает золото"). Available at http://www.vip-volga.narod.ru/taranczev/taranczev.html (as of October 1, 2008).

the Ministry of the Interior.[39] He further shielded himself by building good relations with various national political figures, hosting parties and other events for senior politicians and officials. He even had his picture taken with then Minister of the Interior Anatoly Kulikov.[40]

The pirate markets that Tarantsev controls through his company, Russian Gold, and the company itself are closely connected to organized crime. The firm, established in the early 1990s,[41] worked with another organization after 1993 to become a presence in the lucrative Mitinsky, Tuskinsky, and Pokrovsky markets.[42] As far back as 1998, those markets were handling 3,000 traders and 20,000 customers every day.[43] During that year, the tax police raided Mitinsky and uncovered documents showing it was paying taxes on only 80 million rubles in daily profits, while it actually made 400 million rubles a day.[44]

Reports in 1998 and 2001 noted not only the availability of pirated DVD and CD products, but also the necessity of paying protection in order to sell goods and get advance warning of police raids.[45] On November 21, 2005, a series of police raids (called Operation Counterfeit) were carried out against warehouses and markets, including

---

[39] Leonid Shants, "Alexander Tarantsev: "RUOP is about to destroy me" ("Александр Таранцев: "РУОП Собирается Меня Устранить"), *Profile* (Профиль), March 9, 1998. Available at http://www.profile.ru/items/?item=2068 (as of October 1, 2008).

[40] "Big boy in Moscow, con in Miami," *Moscow News*, December 4, 1997.

[41] Lilia Lagutina, "Alexander Tarantsev: 'I want look the person in the eyes'" ("Александр Таранцев: 'Хочу Смотреть Человеку В Глаза'"), *Trud* (Труд), December 14, 2001. Available at http://www.trud.ru/trud.php?id=200112142300601; "Personal Profile: Alexander Tarantsev" ("Личное дело: Таранцев Александр Петрович"), *Kommersant*, January 18, 2008, available at http://www.kommersant.ru/doc.aspx?DocsID=843186 (as of October 1, 2008); Romanov, "'Russian Gold' does not want to pass for 'Russian Mafia.'" 1997.

[42] Vladislav Trifonov, "General pointed to 'Russian Gold'" ("Генерал показал на 'Русское золото'"), *Kommersant*, January 18, 2008. Available at http://www.kommersant.ru/doc.aspx?DocsID=843044 (as of October 1, 2008).

[43] Julie Tolkacheva, "Addressing the craze for clothes," *The Moscow Times*, May 20, 1994.

[44] "Russian Gold." Available at http://www.opticgifts.info/russian-gold.html

[45] Vladimir Yemelyaneko and Aleksandr Petrov, "21st Century Pirates: Moskovskiye Novosti Correspondents in the Illegal Computer Business," FBIS Document ID: 19980207000193, trans. from *Moskovskiye Novosti* [Moscow], January 25, 1998.

Mitinsky, resulting in the seizure of "hundreds of thousands of pirate discs."[46]

The criminal control that was established over the markets and the efforts to maintain that control led to a spiral of violence that consumed almost everyone involved. Tarantsev is alleged to have ordered several murders for business or personal reasons.[47] The violence reached to rival pirates such as Ayrat Sharipov and Yevgeny Ladik, both of whom were murdered,[48] to makers of DVDs, and to the authorities themselves, as well as interested industry officials, including Konstantine Zemchenkov, head of the Russian Anti-Piracy Organization (RAPO), who was attacked by an unknown gunman believed to be associated with a pirate manufacturing facility being investigated by RAPO, and Vadim Botnaryuk, leader of the Russian Phonographic Association (RPA), who was beaten by two unknown individuals and died of his injuries on January 19, 2008.[49]

Mexico

While Mexico is hardly a stranger to corruption, the protected space for piracy there arose not only from the financial but also the political interests of politicians. The groups amid which piracy was lodged fit the definition of criminals, but they were also part of the constituency of major political actors and parties in Mexico.

---

[46] "Police raid markets and warehouses in 'Operation Counterfeit,'" *WAB*, November 25 – December 1, 2005.

[47] Trifonov, 2008.

[48] "Sharipov murder will affect the CD market" ("Убийство Шарипова повлияет на рынок CD"), *Grani* (Грани), September 29, 2005, available at http://grani.ru/Economy/m.95759. html (translated) (as of October 1, 2008). Gleb Popov, "Black mark for businessman" ("Черная Метка Для Бизнесмена"), *Seventh Capital* (Седьмая Столица), October 17, 2006. Available at http://www.7c.ru/Incidents/4318.html (translated). "Russia: Yuzhnyy Reporter Selection List 9 Oct 06," *BBC Monitoring International Reports*, October 13, 2006.

[49] " Well-known music figure Vadim Botnaryuk dies" ("Скончался известный музыкальный деятель Вадим Ботнарюк"), January 21, 2008. Available at http://www.mk.ru/blogs/ MK/2008/01/21/muzika/334499/ (as of October 1, 2008).

Los Ambulantes[50]

An informal economy of itinerant vendors, called "ambulantes" or "vagoneros," has been a part of Mexico City's cultural fabric for generations.[51] Historically, the ruling party has profited from this economy through an equally informal system of taxation, which might be more accurately described as a system of bribery or extortion.[52] Until recently, regulatory reforms seem to have been enacted with a wink and a nod, largely to appease licensed business owners, and were only sporadically enforced. To strengthen their bargaining power, vendors in Mexico City have coalesced into unions, which have been accused of mafioso tactics.[53] Union leaders negotiate the terms of their agreements with officials, arbitrate internecine disputes, provide social benefits, and exercise their influence, sometimes forcibly, against other groups among the estimated 500,000 street vendors in the city.[54]

- **Highlight.** Protected space for crime arose from a kind of "bargain" between vendors, including those who sold pirated goods, and politicians who wanted not just money but also votes and foot soldiers.
- **Piracy revenue.** Piracy revenue was important to the individual vendors but was not the primary motivation for either their leaders or the politicians.
- **Discovery of piracy.** Pirated goods were a natural and increasingly important element of the vendors' wares and thus were increasingly profitable over time.

---

[50] See Appendix C, pp. 165–177, for a more detailed description of this case.

[51] "Mexico's Illegal Vendors," *NPR Morning Edition*, July 24, 1998.

[52] Stanley Pimental, "The Nexus of Organized Crime and Politics in Mexico," *Trends in Organized Crime*, Vol. 4, No. 3, Spring 1999, pp. 9–28.

[53] Hector Tobar, "Vendor-free zone in Mexico City center," *Los Angeles Times*, October 13, 2007.

[54] Sergio Peña, "Informal Markets: Street Vendors in Mexico City," *Habitat International*, Vol. 23, No. 2, 1999, pp. 363–372.

- **Role of law enforcement.** Enforcement was haphazard, with many authorities on the take and/or acquiescent, perhaps reflecting the stakes of more-senior officials or of the political parties.
- **Evidence base.** The evidence base consists mostly of newspaper or other secondary accounts, supplemented by some official documents.

For more than two decades, Alejandra Barrios was the leader of Mexico City's largest street-vendor organization, the Legitimate Civic and Commercial Association (ALCC).[55] Contrary to the group's name, however, street vending as practiced by the ALCC was not sanctioned by law. Many of the ALCC's 5,000 members sold counterfeit goods, including pirated DVDs, from unlicensed stalls along major pedestrian thoroughfares. (This case focuses on Mexico City, but pirated products are available all over Mexico and are ubiquitous in resort areas.) In the early 1980s, Barrios forged an alliance with the Institutional Revolutionary Party (PRI), which had by then ruled Mexico for more than half a century.[56] Thereafter, the PRI protected the ALCC in exchange for bribes and votes from its membership.[57] ALCC members allegedly even attended political rallies in choreographed shows of support for campaigning officials.[58]

Barrios endured ups and downs, including retribution by authorities against ALCC street vendors when she briefly split from the PRI. She was imprisoned for two years, accused of plotting the murder of the husband of her archrival, Maria Rosette; he was killed during a particularly violent clash between street-vendor groups in 2003.[59]

---

[55] Marla Dickerson, "Mexico's princess and the paupers; A great-grandmother defends the turf of 5,000 street vendors in the capital's core," *Los Angeles Times*, August 13, 2007.

[56] "Hardball politics on the street," *U.S. News and World Report*, July 4, 1988; Dickerson, 2007.

[57] Ibid.

[58] "Hardball politics on the street," 1988.

[59] "Alejandra Barrios: auge y caida," *Proceso*, August 31, 2003.

Despite reports of videotape evidence proving her involvement, Barrios was eventually freed for lack of evidence.[60]

While Barrios was incarcerated, the rival Revolutionary Democratic Party (PRD) came to power, and a new Law of Civic Culture effectively outlawed unlicensed street vending in the city.[61] However, neither the PRD's ascendancy nor the Law of Civic Culture changed the basic bargain in the system, only the players. Rosette led a coalition of street-vendor groups roughly 5,000 members strong, called the Metropolitan Front of Public Vendors' Popular Organizations (MFPVPO). She apparently ran the MFPVPO just as her counterpart, Barrios, ran the ALCC. As of 2006, the PRD was reportedly demanding contributions from its members of 30 pesos a week, raised to 100 pesos a day during campaign season.[62]

Tepito, a slum near the Zócalo (Mexico City's main public square), was once renowned for producing world-class boxing talent but is now notorious for its black market and general lawlessness.[63] It is reportedly because of Tepito that Mexico has the dubious distinction of being the third largest producer of pirated recordings in the world.[64] Imposing order on the neighborhood has proven remarkably difficult. Police raids are met by hurled rocks, bottles, and Molotov cocktails.[65] In 2003, the neighborhood repelled 1,200 elite police backed by helicopters and armored vehicles.[66]

Tepito's resistance to law enforcement makes it terrain for fencing and piracy and provides a haven for the more dangerous crimi-

---

[60] Arturo Paramo, "Absorbe PRD-DF a los ambulantes," *Reforma*, May 22, 2005; Arturo Paramo, "Va Alejandra Barrios de vuleta a las calles," *Reforma*, December 16, 2005.

[61] Claudia Bolaños, Rubelio Fernández, and Icela Lagunas, "Rechazan la ley cívica 'armados' con sus franelas," *El Universal*, August 12, 2004.

[62] "Enviada especial," *El País*, June 21, 2006; "Ambulantes pagan a grupos del PRD $15 millones al mes," *México Sí*. Available at http://mexico.blogsome.com/2006/12/20/

[63] Ibsen Martinez, "Tepito's Way," *The Library of Economics and Liberty*, October 3, 2005.

[64] Ibid.; "Enviada especial," *El País*, June 21, 2006.

[65] Ginger Thompson, "In Mexico, a man with a badge isn't a good guy," *New York Times*, November 24, 2000.

[66] Martinez, 2005.

nal enterprises of narcotics and arms trafficking. Drive-by shootings have become commonplace.[67] The Tijuana drug cartel once was said to be ensconced in the neighborhood, using local children to distribute cocaine throughout the capital.[68] The Federal Investigation Agency (AFI) led an early morning anti-piracy raid of warehouses in Tepito in October 2006, confiscating tons of discs and 300 burners capable of producing 43,200 pirated DVDs per day.[69] To illustrate what a cesspool of crime Tepito became, according to authoritative press accounts, six raids were made between April and July 2008, one of which resulted in the seizure of 150 tons of counterfeit material.[70] By late 2006, when Mexican President Felipe Calderon moved to evict residents and street vendors from Tepito, it had become Mexico's premier "narco-neighborhood."

Strains of the drama that played out in the streets of Mexico City echoed in its subway system, where an estimated 40,000-plus vendors have been organized into 16 groups, the most notorious of which goes by the innocuous name Ángeles Metropolitanos and is led by Alejandro Casabal Flores. The groups hawk pirated discs and battle for dominance of the various train lines.[71] Although protective political alliances are not as overt as those aboveground, a similar pattern of inconsistent enforcement and judicial irregularities is suggestive of a somewhat similar bargain. Not only have vendors disregarded the law and obstructed the corridors of the trains and stations with their wares,

---

[67] Thompson, 2000.

[68] Martinez, 2005; "Illicit drug lab closed down," *The News*, May 30, 2001.

[69] "Desmantela AFI laboratorio de piratería," *Agencias*, October 18, 2006.

[70] These were: July 15, 2008 (30 tons seized), http://www.radiotrece.com.mx/2007/07/26/decomisan-30-toneladas-de-pirateria-en-tepito/; July 10, 2008, http://www.terra.com.mx/articulo.aspx?articuloId=698774; June 19, 2008 (5 tons), http://www.eluniversal.com.mx/notas/516101.html; June 10, 2008 (10 tons), http://radiomixteca.com.mx/noticias/?p=331; May 17, 2008 (7 tons), http://mx.news.yahoo.com; April 23, 2008 (150 tons), http://www.elsiglodetorreon.com.mx/noticia/346585.aseguran-150-toneladas-de-pirateria-en-tepito.html (all websites available as of October 1, 2008).

[71] "Mapa delictivo de los vagoneros del Metro," *Noticias Televisa*, February 1, 2006.

they have been involved in violent physical altercations with both rival vendors and police.[72]

Enforcement of the law against DVD piracy—and unauthorized Metro vending in general—has been erratic. A staggering number of Metro vendors have been fined since the Civic Culture Law was enacted: 10,674 street vendors were sent before civic judges in 2004, and the number grew to 24,194 in 2005, with another 42,797 evicted from the Metro without being cited.[73] Officials have implored Metro riders not to buy pirated DVDs and have pledged repeatedly to use a *mano duro* (hard hand) to deter Ángeles Metropolitanos.[74] And yet, the day after one such proclamation, Metro vendors were selling with impunity in plain view of authorities.[75] Shortly thereafter, 15 transit security officers were fired for allegedly looking the other way as Ángeles Metropolitanos hawked their wares.[76]

Although Flores, known on the street as "El Tuercas," has denied that his organization enjoys any political support,[77] he has been freed three times within days of his arrests, for reasons that invite skepticism.[78] He was also pardoned by prosecutors after a domestic-abuse charge.[79] One judge dismissed charges because they were based entirely on victim testimony, even though one of those victims was a police

---

[72] *Liberan El Tuercas después de 9 días de ingresar al Reclusorio Oriente*, Boletín Informativo Núm. 4, Secretaría de Seguridad Publica del Distrito Federal, January 1, 2006; Angel Bolaños and Erika Duarte, "Rebasan vagoneros la vigilancia en el STC-Metro, reconoce la directora," *La Jornada*, December 10, 2005.

[73] Bolaños and Duarte, 2005.

[74] Ibid.; Laura Gomez Flores, "STC: No habrá cuartel en la lucha contra los vagoneros," *La Jornada*, January 23, 2006.

[75] Mael Vallejo, "Permiten policías vendera los vagoneros," *La Crónica de Hoy*, December 10, 2005.

[76] Flores, 2006.

[77] Agustin Salgado, "Vagoneros del metro denuncian abusos policiacos," *La Jornada*, October 16, 2004.

[78] Miguel Nila Cedillo, "Sale Alejandro Casabal Flores en libertad del Reclusorio Oriente," *Once Noticias*, January 2, 2006.

[79] Hector Molina, "El Tuercas evadía la prisión cambiando su identidad," *El Universal*, December 19, 2005.

auxiliary officer.[80] If the bargain that creates protected space for the subway vendors is less visible than that for street vendors, it still seems to operate.

Japan

The *yakuza*, descendants of medieval gamblers and outlaws, grew into a cohesive force in the late 19th and early 20th centuries. In Japan's modernization, the *yakuza* (known more broadly as the *boryokudan*) came to be regarded as contemporary samurai, a masterless criminal class bound by a tradition of honor and duty. Their alliances with right-wing ultranationalist groups afforded them protection and acceptance among Japan's generally conservative population.[81] As the country rebuilt its infrastructure after World War II, the *yakuza* formed a working alliance with the Liberal Democratic Party and were tacitly given a legitimate role, that of ensuring order on the streets and enabling a flourishing black market.[82] This relationship endured for the next 50 years, sending down deep roots of corruption across Japanese political, law enforcement, and civil institutions.

It was the *yakuza's* symbiotic relationship with the police that ensured its members' survival as a protected species of criminal in Japan. During Japan's post-World War II reconstruction, the *yakuza* held the balance of power on the street and helped the nation's struggling police force gain territorial intelligence and fill in the gaps of its command. Even after a police force had gained control of a territory, the *yakuza* was often summoned to help keep the area orderly.[83] There was ultimately little doubt about who the *yakuza* members were in a

---

[80] Leticia Fernandez, "Liberan bajo fianza a cinco 'vagoneros,'" *Reforma*, February 14, 2006.

[81] Mark Galeotti, "Yakuza splits into 'white-collar' and violent crime," *Jane's Intelligence Review,* June 1, 2001.

[82] Peter Hill, "The Changing Face of the Yakuza," *Global Crime,* Vol. 6, No. 1, February 2004, p. 112.

[83] Ibid., p. 98.

given community; for decades, gangs would submit membership lists to the National Police Agency (NPA).[84] From 1957 to 1999, the historical average was one *yakuza* member for every 1,000 members of the population.[85]

However, by the early 1990s, the public mood had turned sharply against the *yakuza*. Although the origins of Japan's economic downturn lay squarely in the failure of the white (legitimate) market, the *yakuza's* role in the economic crisis was unmistakable. Decades of corruption had eroded the nation's civil institutions and had given rise to drug trafficking and gun violence that eventually caught the police, the *yakuza's* tacit allies, in the crossfire.[86] As the economy deteriorated, public tolerance of the gangs eroded. Many dubbed the troubles "a *yakuza* recession," placing blame on the havoc the gangs wreaked on financial institutions and national corporations.[87]

In response, the Japanese Diet unanimously passed the *boryokudan* countermeasures, which came into effect in 1992.[88] The legislation included anti-racketeering statutes that lowered the definition of intimidation, effectively criminalizing the *yakuza's* use of its "reputation for violence" as the instrument for achieving its members' demands. On the whole, Japan's measures were mild compared with Hong Kong's anti-triad laws or the U.S. RICO statute, but they did give police the right to close *yakuza* offices in times of emergency, and they prohibited the display of the gangs' insignia.

---

[84] Galeotti, 2001.

[85] Curtis J. Milhaupt and Mark D. West, "The Dark Side of Private Ordering: An Institutional and Empirical Analysis of Organized Crime," *University of Chicago Law Review*, Vol. 67, 2000, p. 41.

[86] David E. Kaplan and Alec Dubro, *Yakuza: Japan's Criminal Underworld*, Berkeley, CA: University of California Press, 2003, p. 328.

[87] Hill, 2004, p. 105.

[88] Ibid., p. 102.

Yakuza: Yamaguchi-gumi[89]

On September 22, 2006, more than 150 police officers moved in on the Nihonbashi area of Osaka to shut down a network of more than 21 pirate-DVD street vendors. Police analysis revealed that both the territory and the piracy activity were controlled by four affiliates of the Yamaguchi-gumi, Japan's largest organized-crime syndicate. While these street-level gangs operated their illicit activities underground, their leaders led (and continue to lead) very visible lives, with clearly marked offices and biographies published in *yakuza*-themed magazines sold in newsstands across Japan.

- **Highlight.** Despite a crackdown on Japan's major organized-crime syndicates, the *yakuza*, prior decades of tolerance of the gangs by politicians, police, and the public allow a protected space for crimes such as piracy to exist in an afterglow of corruption.
- **Piracy revenue.** In 2005, piracy revenue became a major source of income for several affiliate gangs of the Yamaguchi-gumi that controlled rackets in Nihonbashi, a neighborhood of southern Osaka.
- **Discovery of piracy.** The gangs' transition into piracy follows the decline in revenues for *yakuza* gangs from illegal pornographic DVDs that was caused by widespread availability of Internet pornography.
- **Role of law enforcement.** Japan's law enforcement community has taken important steps to monitor the *yakuza's* involvement in intellectual-property crimes. Japan's National Police Agency keeps official statistics on *yakuza* members engaged in piracy, as do prefecture police departments.
- **Evidence base.** The evidence base is compiled from extensive interviews with multiple police agencies (some on the record and some off), corroborated by press accounts and industry newsletters.

That an organized-crime group could lead such a public existence is a paradox explained only by years of tolerance on the part of Japan's

---

[89] See Appendix C, pp. 118–140, for a more detailed description of this case.

politicians, police, and public. The paradox is all the more surprising given that Japan, unlike Russia, is a thriving democracy and, unlike Mexico, prides itself on its orderly civil and political institutions. Transparency International ranks Japan among the top 20 countries in the world for eliminating corruption, ahead of the United States and France.[90] Moreover, in comparison with most countries in Asia, Japan enjoys a low piracy rate (estimated losses of around 15 percent of company revenues) and takes piracy enforcement seriously. In January 2007, the country used its strictest Organized Crime Punishment Law to prosecute three "ordinary" pirates who had no *yakuza* connections.[91]

The persistence of gangs in Japan points to the protected spaces that remain because *yakuza* are so firmly entrenched in Japanese society. Indeed, police pressure in the 1990s, like that in the 1960s, might actually have pushed the gangs to consolidate.[92,93] Today, the three major *yakuza* syndicates—Yamaguchi-gumi, Sumiyoshi-kai and Inagawa-kai—account for 73 percent of total *yakuza* membership and work almost as an oligopoly in the underworld of crime.[94]

The *yakuza* have also become more international, establishing working arrangements with regional triad groups in China, Hong Kong, and Macao for the supply of narcotics and money-laundering facilities. *Yakuza* members have also set up regional outposts as bases for illegal businesses. In 2004, police arrested Yamaguchi-gumi's lead Taiwanese representative for running a pirate satellite business that

---

[90] Japan scored a 17 on Transparency International's 2007 Corruption Perceptions Index. Available at http://www.transparency.org/policy_research/surveys_indices/cpi/2007 (as of July 10, 2008)

[91] "Organized Crime Punishment Law used for first time to target copyright infringers in Japan," Japan and International Motion Picture Copyright Association, press release, July 30, 2007.

[92] Foreign Broadcast Information Service, *Asahi: Cover Story/Tokyo's Turf,* FBIS Document ID: JPP20051007969014, *Tokyo Asahi Shimbun* (Internet version-WWW) in English, October 7, 2005.

[93] Hill, 2004, p. 99.

[94] Peter Hill, "Heisei Yakuza: Burst Bubble and Botaiho" *Social Science Japan Journal,* Vol. 6, No. 1, 2003, p. 12.

beamed illegal pornographic videos to subscribers in Taiwan, Japan, Korea, Guam, and several Southeast Asian countries. In less than two years, the business had garnered more than $10 million in revenue and had demonstrated the technological skills of the *yakuza* gangs.[95]

Under increased scrutiny from police, the higher ranks of these organizations work to keep a façade of respectability for their semi-legitimate business and charitable activity. As a result, the gangs continue to enjoy a public face. For instance, when the chairman of the Yamaguchi-gumi retired in 2005, his replacement's succession ceremony was covered live on national news.[96] *Yakuza* black market business earnings alone are estimated at over $10 billion, and forays into legitimate markets raise the number still higher.[97]

Many members in the lowest ranks have not been able to make the transition to legitimate operations. Smaller gangs either have gone out of business or have been subsumed into the larger gangs. At the street level, the *yakuza* have essentially "franchised" to these smaller groups traditional mainstay criminal activities such as racketeering, gambling, loan-sharking, and narcotics trafficking, as well as newer crimes such as piracy and counterfeiting. This move has allowed higher-level *yakuza* members to disassociate themselves from vice but still have a profit stake in illicit activities, such as the methamphetamine market in Japan, which, at 600,000 addicts and 2.18 million casual users, is one of the largest illicit operations in Asia.[98]

In these circumstances, piracy has been a natural part of *yakuza* criminal portfolios, since illicit street vending was always a core criminal activity for the gangs. One survey found that the most common

---

[95] Foreign Broadcast Information Service, "Japan, Taiwan Gangsters Arrested for Satellite Pornography," FBIS Document ID: CPP20041021000149, Taipei, *The China Post* (Internet Version-WWW) in English, October 21, 2004, "Taiwan" page.

[96] Mark Galeotti, "Japanese yakuza consolidation risks strife in Tokyo," *Jane's Intelligence Review*, November 1, 2005.

[97] Eric Johnston, "Yakuza in Japan: From rackets to real estate, yakuza mutltifacted," *Japan Times,* February 14, 2007. Available at http://search.japantimes.co.jp/cgi-bin/nn20070214i1.html (as of October 1, 2008).

[98] Galeotti, 2001.

businesses of *yakuza* members were street stalls (5,552 surveyed members), followed by lending agencies (3,239), bars (3,129), strip clubs and spas (2,692), restaurants (2,596), and construction firms (2,171).[99] Moreover, international connections, the growing sophistication of the gangs, and the low barrier to entry into piracy have driven some gangs directly into manufacturing. Police reports reflect a growing awareness of *yakuza* connections to piracy and counterfeiting. A 2004 National Police report on *yakuza* economic crimes cited the fact that police had concluded 19 investigations of IPR theft involving *yakuza* gangs and detained some 32 suspects. Overall, IPR theft ranked among the top five economic crimes committed by the *yakuza*, behind loan-sharking and illegal waste disposal. A 2006 National Police Agency report on IPR crimes cited 43 cases linked to *yakuza* members, comprising almost 9 percent of all IPR crimes committed that year.[100] In interviews, police sources cautioned that these national statistics understate *yakuza* involvement in piracy. According to the police, the number is far higher.[101]

Many piracy enterprises were offshoots of illegal pornography operations that had been a long-time source of revenue for *yakuza* gangs.[102] Underground pornography operations were an important source of revenue for the Rakudaime Yamaguchi-gumi affiliate Oharagumi, complementing their other activities. The price of an illegal pornographic DVD was often three times that of a pirate film. Yet once Internet pornography became increasingly profitable in Japan, profits from these hard-goods ventures decreased. Piracy of mainstream films

[99] Norikiyo Hayashi and Soshiki Boryoku, 1996, as cited in Milhaupt and West, 2000, p. 29.

[100] National Police Agency Japan, "Countermeasures against IPR counterfeiting and piracy," February 2007. Available at www.npa.go.jp/safetylife/seikan36/20070308.pdf (as of July 10, 2008).

[101] Interview with Police Superintendent Hisashi Takagi, Osaka Prefecture Police Department, November 17, 2006.

[102] Some forms of pornography are permitted in Japan. However, hard-core or explicit pornography is illegal, and there is a flourishing black market in these goods.

became a natural progression for the gangs, such as the Ohara-gumi, as a way to build new revenue streams.[103]

All of the mercantile and illicit activities of Osaka converge at Nihonbashi. The northern end of the area is a thriving hub for electronic retailers. Many of these shops discreetly sell illegal pornographic DVDs out of back rooms for *yakuza* gangs. The southern area, full of bars and hotels, is a hub for prostitution, narcotics, and more-overt pornography vending. Overlaid on this illicit activity is an extensive *yakuza* racket that has been in place since World War II.

Following intensive analysis and interrogation of the September 22 piracy suspects, the Osaka Prefectural Police officially concluded that the spike in piracy activity in Nihonbashi was a direct result of *yakuza* involvement in the area.[104] Intelligence analysis developed a clear picture of the chain of command between the different syndicate members. Most fascinating was the overlap of various *yakuza* gang affiliations, with gangsters working for one gang leader but paying tribute to his rival. Police analysts concluded that the logic behind this web of tribute payments was a division of labor.

The gangs continue to have a very visible public presence. Extensive features written about the president of the Hayano-kai and the president of the Ohara-gumi can be found published in *yakuza*-focused magazines that are distributed at most major newsstands in Japan. Succession pacts and internal gang politics are chronicled almost the way celebrity activities are in fan magazines. In the 2006 Yamaguchi-gumi yearbook, the president of the Ohara-gumi was lauded for his role in rushing relief supplies to 1995 Kobe earthquake survivors and was described as a "godfather type with sincere social obligations and people skills." Finally, it is still quite easy to locate *yakuza*-gang offices. The offices are clearly marked with the gang's symbol, and despite ominous security measures, the gangs make no apparent attempt to mask their presence.

---

[103] Interview with Police Superintendent Hisashi Takagi, Osaka Prefecture Police Department, November 17, 2006.

[104] Ibid.

There is a strong argument that *yakuza* membership is not simply symbolic, but that it confers real benefits in the criminal underworld. As this case study demonstrates, affiliations between Yamaguchi-gumi gangs paved the way for cooperation in a highly competitive piracy market. Police attest to the fact that *yakuza* gangs were able to force out or tax other vendors from the area (primarily amateur Israeli piracy vendors) precisely because of the perceived threat the *yakuza* pose.[105]

The *yakuza* still benefit from a discernible afterglow of corruption in Japan. Years of acceptance on the part of politicians, police, and the public have perhaps forced the upper elites of *yakuza* gangs to evolve into socially acceptable, less overtly criminal individuals. Yet the leadership continues to enable protected space for street-level gangs and, as a result, makes it all the more difficult to counter piracy and other crimes with which it is nested.

The Bottom Line

That many governments are corrupt at many levels is unremarkable. So, too, is the likelihood that corruption will increase with the profits of criminal enterprises. Yet because corruption is often less subtle in other countries than it is in the United States, it is easy to overlook the subtler forms it may take. Protected spaces for crime arise in Russia, Mexico, and many other countries in part because of obvious corruption, authorities paid to turn a blind eye. But protected spaces also arise because of the stakes of politicians and their interactions with their constituencies.[106] To be sure, overt corruption is an abiding check on the ability of public authorities to crack down on counterfeiting or film

---

[105]Confirmed with Osaka Police Department sources.

[106]From 2001 to 2007, the United States ranked between 16th and 20th on Transparency International's Corruption Perception Index, behind Northern Europe, Singapore, Hong Kong, and Canada. Mexico has gone from 51st to 72nd, and Russia from 79th to 143rd, as the number of nations surveyed has increased from 91 to 179. The complete rankings and the survey methodology are available at http://www.transparency.org/policy_research/surveys_indices/cpi (as of October 1, 2008).

piracy. Even when political will is present or seems to be, especially at the top of governments, the real capacity to act may not be present, particularly at the local level. The next chapter discusses enforcement in the context of strategy and choice—how nations decide to deploy their law enforcement resources.

CHAPTER SEVEN

Innovations in Enforcement

Since the face of film piracy is uglier than is often recognized, how should national policy and law enforcement respond? What more could be done? And, given scarce resources, what more should be done to dry up this source of funding for organized-crime syndicates and terrorist organizations?

DVD film piracy is a lucrative part of the portfolios of organized crime and can fund violent crime, including terrorism. As a crime, film piracy devalues respect for law and order, and its distribution points can become havens or protected spaces for still other crimes. Buying a pirated film often abets criminal organizations, some of which are engaged in drug trafficking or human smuggling, or worse, and which are hardly above using violence to protect their turf and their criminal franchises.

Challenges to Increasing the Priority of Piracy

The reasons enforcement authorities might not devote high-priority attention to counterfeiting in general or film piracy in particular have been mentioned throughout this report and can be summarized briefly here. The question now, though, is how this situation should change given the strong evidence that organized crime has embraced counterfeiting and that some terrorist groups also appear to benefit from money made through counterfeiting. Should more resources be devoted to combating counterfeiting? And in any case, how might existing enforcement resources be better deployed to provide better intelligence about organized crime and terrorism, to lead to the apprehension of leaders, and to dry up this lucrative source of funding for them?

Government Will Is Limited

The first challenge is that government will to devote significant resources to policing counterfeiting is limited. That is not true everywhere, as illustrated by cases as far-flung as Hong Kong, Malaysia, and England; nor is it true all across the United States, as underscored by discussion of New York and Los Angeles below. But so long as the image persists that counterfeiting is a victimless crime, the case for vigorous enforcement seems limited, all the more so because counterfeiting is a *complicit* crime, one that links willing sellers and buyers. Other counterfeited goods, such as fraudulent pharmaceuticals or low-quality machinery, present a more urgent risk to public safety, but pirated DVDs lack those arguments. In these circumstances, it is tempting to think that low-level enforcement operations do little more than harass hapless peddlers—who may themselves be victims.

Serious investigation to uncover the links between piracy and organized crime is challenged by the transnational nature of many of the counterfeiting operations. Globalization has opened up new markets and opportunities for criminal networks and IPR infringement. The continual improvement of communications technology and the reduction of national trade barriers encourage transnational trade but at the same time challenge law enforcement, which must still work through traditional systems of international legal cooperation.

In some countries, the prevailing attitude seems to be that foreign multinational corporations should not be entitled to IPR protection. For instance, in 2001, a member of the Kenyan Parliament bought a legitimate DVD for Sh3,000 and used it to demonstrate that stores in the business district were fleecing the public, since an illegitimate copy could have been bought elsewhere for Sh400.[1] In Russia, a judge declined to sentence a teacher who was convicted of using a bootlegged copy of Microsoft Windows, stating that the damage the

---

[1] "Kenya: Pirates' Paradise," *Africa News*, February 10, 2006.

teacher caused Microsoft was insignificant compared with Microsoft's overall earnings.[2]

Not only are pirated DVDs in developing countries considerably cheaper than legitimate DVDs, in some countries it is difficult even to find the latter. In Iraq, Multinational Force-Iraq forward operating bases even have officially permitted shops that sell pirated DVDs and sometimes little else. Legitimate DVDs can be bought only in the exchanges on larger bases. There will always be demand for cheap entertainment, even though the quality of pirated versions varies widely. In Eastern Europe, state-owned enterprises have engaged in counterfeiting, and in poor countries, some piracy reflects entrepreneurial activity where few people can pay the prices for legitimate DVDs.

Moreover, producing counterfeit goods may be an important source of income in poor areas, making it less likely that law enforcement officers will be motivated to crack down on counterfeiting operations.[3] As stated by Luis Munurriaga, the district attorney of Ciudad del Este, Paraguay: "We can't go after just anyone. Poor people here depend on jobs linked to this business to survive. But when companies complain, we have to take action."[4] In Malaysia, when officials attempted to raid a counterfeiting factory, they were met at the plant by an angry mob that refused to let them enter, just like the crowds in Tepito that resisted raids by the authorities.[5]

Even if police do close down a piracy operation, the investment in a DVD-burning operation is so low that the operation may start up again quickly. Pressing machines involve considerably more overhead; however, in a number of instances, apparently legitimate factories have been found to be producing licensed DVDs some of the time

[2] Andrew Kramer, "Russian Judge Waives Software Piracy Penalty," *International Herald Tribune*, February 15, 2007, p. 11.

[3] Eric Priest, "The Future of Music and Film Piracy in China," *Berkeley Technology Law Journal*, Vol. 21, No. 2, 2006, p. 822.

[4] Benedict Mander, "Glimmer of success in Paraguay's corruption battle," *Financial Times*, August 15, 2006, p. 6.

[5] Shi-Ian Lee, "Lucky, Flo sniff through charcoal to a RM1M haul," *New Strait Times*, April 15, 2007.

but "moonlighting" by producing pirated DVDs at other times, so the legitimate operation can continue, and the moonlighting operation may reboot when law enforcement attention wanes or authorities avert their gaze because of corruption, as the Russian cases show. The cost of the product itself is so low that a loss of inventory is fairly insignificant. Raided shops continually reopen: The Beijing Yongsheng Century International Cultural Co. has been "raided so often—at least fourteen times since 2005—that it's acquired the nickname 'Dan's Shop,' after Dan Glickman, chief executive of the Motion Picture Association of America."[6]

Law Enforcement Resources Are Limited

Even if the will of government to devote high-priority attention to counterfeiting is there, the capacity may not be. Like all public agencies, the activities of law enforcement agencies are constrained by mandates and resources. Policing agencies are perennially short of funding to some degree. Within a framework of limited resources, politics and leadership control law enforcement agencies' policing priorities. Given the attitudes and economic factors described above, police in a wide array of jurisdictions will devote at best a limited portion of their resources to enforcing IPR rules. Even then, the priority will be to police counterfeits that present hazards to public safety and health.

In the developing world, police departments starved for funding encourage corruption by paying such poor wages to officers that they are encouraged to supplement their income. While police officers in developed countries might supplement their incomes by working overtime on security details, it is common in the developing world for police officers to shake down citizens or offer their services to criminal organizations, as the cases in Chapter Six demonstrate all too vividly.[7]

---

[6] Dawn C. Chmielewski, "Film not out yet on DVD? You can find it in China," *Los Angeles Times*, November 12, 2007. Available at http://www.latimes.com/business/ (as of October 1, 2008).

[7] Jeremiah Goulka and Stephen Nelleman, "Drugged Law Enforcement: The Influence of Drug Trafficking on Human Rights and the Rule of Law in Mexico," in William Cartwright (ed.), *Mexico: Facing the Challenges of Human Rights and Crime*, Ardsley, NY: Transnational Publishers, 1999, pp. 23–39.

The mandate of customs agencies to crack down on counterfeiting varies. Hong Kong polices aggressively, as the cases indicate, whereas Canada has a limited legislative mandate. In Canada, border officials do not have the power to seize counterfeit goods; that requires a police presence or a detention order obtained by the holder of the rights—the latter unlikely because the rights holders rarely know ahead of time what material is crossing the border. Moreover, once goods are detained, the police or rights holder must seek an additional court order to determine the legality of the products. The absence of an effective system for enforcing IPR at the Canadian border results in a huge amount of counterfeit product entering the country, especially when there is no reason to believe that those products pose a significant health or safety threat.[8] This is one of the factors that earned Canada the dubious honor of being the only OECD country on the International Intellectual Property Association's watch list for failing to implement World Intellectual Property Organization (WIPO) standards. In the words of one prominent IPR organization, "Canada remains far behind virtually all its peers in the industrialized world with respect to its efforts to bring its copyright laws up to date."[9]

Stricter Law Enforcement

As the message becomes clearer that piracy is not a victimless crime and that it provides money that can be used for other criminal enterprises—and for terrorism—a number of countries are making serious efforts to address counterfeiting, and not just those, like the United States, Britain, and Hong Kong, that have major film and other IPR-based industries to protect. Taiwan and Malaysia, for instance, recently established special courts to manage IPR-related litigation within their

---

[8] Iain Marlow, "Dangerous fake goods cross border unchallenged: Agency has no power to seize items but fear over Chinese imports could change that," *Toronto Star*, July 2, 2007, p. A1.

[9] International Intellectual Property Alliance, *Special 301 Report*, 2007, p. 10. Available at http://www.iipa.com/2007_SPEC301_TOC.htm (as of September 28, 2008).

territories; these courts are meant to shorten the time between accusation and trial and to encourage the development of IPR-related expertise among the judiciary.

Recognizing the Link

A number of countries and international bodies have taken note of the link between organized crime and IPR offenses and as a result have sought to increase attention to IPR crimes:

- In 1996, the United States became one of the first countries to incorporate copyright offenses into anti-organized-crime statutes. Under 18 U.S.C. § 1961(1)(B), Congress expanded the definition of racketeering activity to include three predicate acts of copyright infringement.
- In 1997, the G-8 Senior Experts on Transnational Organized Crime (Lyon Group) included in its official 40 recommendations a recommendation that the World Customs Organization (WCO) extend its support in the fight against new-technology crimes. A landmark memorandum of understanding between the WCO and the MPA was signed in August 1997 to pave the way for better IPR enforcement against transnational organized-crime syndicates.
- In 2000, the United Nations Convention Against Transnational Organized Crime (Palermo Convention) reasserted the importance of Interpol in the fight against organized crime. One hundred twenty-four countries signed the convention, and in the following months, Interpol held its first conference on combating counterfeiting and established the Interpol Intellectual Property Crime Action Group (IPCAG) to coordinate police anti-counterfeiting action across jurisdictions.
- In 2002, the British National Criminal Intelligence Service (NCIS) listed IPR theft in its annual national threat assessment and deemed it an easily exploitable source of funding for organized-crime syndicates.
- In 2003, the OECD's Financial Action Task Force (FATF) amended its 30 anti-money-laundering recommendations to

include (1) copyright offenses as categorical offenses and (2) predicate crimes of money laundering.

- In 2004, a task force established by U.S. Attorney General John Ashcroft proposed a series of sweeping changes to IPR enforcement, including seven recommendations on international cooperation to target transnational organized-crime networks involved in counterfeiting and piracy.
- In 2005, the U.S. Trade Representative and the U.S. Departments of Commerce, Justice, and Homeland Security continued to advance their Strategy Targeting Organized Piracy (STOP!), pledging to introduce IPR initiatives within multilateral organizations such as the G-8, the OECD, and Asia-Pacific Economic Cooperation (APEC).
- In 2005, the U.S. Commerce Department created a new position, Coordinator of International Intellectual Property Enforcement, to coordinate interagency anti-piracy efforts to develop policies that address international intellectual-property violations and enforce intellectual-property laws overseas.

Stepped-Up Enforcement: The Case of Hong Kong

Hong Kong is a striking instance of stepped-up enforcement. Hong Kong officials are given the authority to carry on counterfeiting investigations much longer than typical operations, in some cases well over a year. The Organized and Serious Crime Ordinance (Cap 455) (OSCO) was amended in 2000 to include counterfeiting and copyright offenses. Its authorization of extensive witness- and document-production orders, as well as far-reaching search warrants, has been particularly useful in breaking the "wall of silence" that keeps victims and witnesses from cooperating with investigators.[10] Stiffer sentencing guidelines, money-laundering offenses, and asset-forfeiture provisions allow prosecutors greater latitude to keep syndicate leaders off the street longer and have the proceeds of their crimes frozen; they also provide those arrested

---

[10] Jonathan Dotan, interview with with Albert Chan, Chief Hong Kong Customs and Excise Special Task Force, August 17, 2005; Anny Wong, interviews with Hong Kong Customs and Excise officials, November 30, 2007.

with more incentive to cooperate with authorities in pursuit of reduced sentences.

This sustained, aggressive crackdown on DVD piracy, including manufacturing and sales operations, has all but put out of business many of the smaller organized-crime groups, those composed of only a few people.[11] Not surprisingly, cracking down on the large groups is much more difficult, because the big bosses insulate themselves from the organization. When affiliates are destroyed, that is simply part of the cost of doing business; in any event, those affiliates might not even be able to name the big criminal bosses banking their piracy operations or collecting extortion fees from them. Gangs are said to launder their money through the film industry in Hong Kong, and actors have claimed that 90 percent of the industry is controlled by the triads.

Changing technology and the changing "business" models of disc piracy will continue to challenge law enforcement, which risks finding itself not only limited by resources but also constrained by laws and expertise in fighting counterfeiters. The Hong Kong government's actions to empower enforcement officers—especially HKC&E—are an excellent example of efforts to combat movie and music piracy. However, it will clearly take a sustained and aggressive effort involving experienced and well-trained professionals to make a difference. Part of the success they achieve must also be attributed to the fact that continuing economic growth in Hong Kong allows many more people to be able to afford to pay more for legal DVDs. Proximity to Shenzhen, China, also means that individual travelers can bring back to Hong Kong pirated or lower-cost China-version discs for personal consumption instead of purchasing from vendors in Hong Kong.

It is important to note that the numbers of patents, trademarks, and copyrights registered by Chinese companies and individuals have been rising rapidly over the past few years, and since 2005, China has been among the top ten filers of international patents with WIPO.[12] As the portion of China's economy that has a stake in IPR grows, China is

---

[11] Jonathan Dotan, interviews with local authorities in Hong Kong, August 17, 2005.

[12] Heoeng Jia, "China joins top ten for international patents," *SciDev.net*, February 7, 2006, Available at http://www.scidev.net/news/index.cfm (as of December 24, 2007).

likely to become more aggressive in protecting its IPR and prosecuting counterfeiters. Foreign IPR holders are also likely to benefit.

Meanwhile, some degree of IPR cooperation between the United States and China has begun. In 2003, U.S. Immigration and Customs Enforcement launched the joint "Operation Spring" in cooperation with Chinese law enforcement, the first joint cooperation between U.S. and Chinese officials to pursue a crackdown on piracy in both countries. [13] The operation successfully resulted in the 2004 arrest of Randolph Guthrie III and several co-conspirators who were running a large-scale film-piracy business in China.

These are positive steps forward, but it will take more to counter de facto state assistance to counterfeiters. The encouragement states give to IPR pirates is usually not overt, but passive, characterized by inaction and the resulting creation of protected spaces for crime. Few resources are devoted to law enforcement efforts to crack down on counterfeiting, sentences are minimal, seized goods are often returned, and border controls are loose. Until this situation changes, occasional sting operations and prosecutions will net only the small operators, perhaps increasing the control of major organized-crime groups.

If countries do choose to use law enforcement to crack down on counterfeiting, what type of sentence will be an effective deterrent? The World Trade Organization's (WTO's) Agreement on Trade-Related Aspects of Intellectual Property Rights Agreement (TRIPS) states that "remedies available shall include imprisonment and/or monetary fines sufficient to provide a deterrent," but what will actually deter?[14] In general, the United States tends to impose longer terms of incarceration than most European countries.

The fact that penalties for IPR crimes in most countries are modest reduces both the deterrent effect of law enforcement and the willingness of those arrested to cooperate in pursuing an investigation. Experienced criminals know that the likelihood of being arrested for

---

[13] Julie Myers "Testimony by Julie Meyers, Assistant Secretary, U.S. Department of Homeland Security," Customs Budget Authorization, Committee on House Ways and Means Subcommittee on Trade, *LexisNexis Congressional*, July 25, 2006.

[14] TRIPS, article 61.

counterfeiting in general or DVD piracy in particular is miniscule. Yet fashioning penalties that would be effective will run into issues of proportionality and human rights. For instance, it would be inappropriate to recommend stiff penalties in a country known for its human rights abuses in prison.[15] Some countries in the developing world mete out harsh punishments for even relatively minor crimes, with a few such as Afghanistan under the Taliban reaching extremes that exceeded common notions of human rights. What types of sentencing for international organized crime involved in piracy would deter those who had already experienced the brutality of incarceration in a country with little regard for human rights?[16]

Industries that are victims of IPR crimes have developed partnerships with law enforcement officials worldwide. Investigations by industry supplement what local law enforcement authorities can or are prepared to do, including providing information to law enforcement that lead to successful investigations and raids and providing training in techniques for investigating and prosecuting IPR crimes.[17] IPR advocates could step up current efforts to invest in or collaborate with local IPR-based industries to help build a local constituency that supports IPR protections. They could also collaborate with non-governmental organizations (NGOs) to fight corruption and promote transparency. And they could assist that constituency with training for industry, advocacy groups, and judges.

---

[15] TRIPS recognizes the need for proportionality but avoids the issue of human rights violations by stating that available remedies must be "sufficient to provide a deterrent" but also "consistent with the level of penalties applied for crimes of a corresponding gravity" (Article 61).

[16] This is a problem faced by American law enforcement generally in regard to foreign organized crime operating in the United States. For instance, conversations with the Glendale, California Police Department regarding their efforts to police the Armenian Power gang make clear that gang and Armenian Mafia leaders are unfazed by American prisons, governed by the Eighth Amendment, which pale in comparison to their brutal experiences in Armenian prisons.

[17] See Jeffrey Scott McIllwain, "Intellectual Property Theft and Organized Crime: The Case of Film Piracy," *Trends in Organized Crime*, Vol. 8, No. 4, 2005.

Stepped-Up Enforcement: The Cases of NYPD and LAPD

New York and Los Angeles are home to a huge array of IPR-based companies in industries that are threatened by counterfeiting, such as film, music, and fashion. Given the local importance of these industries, these cities have made policing counterfeiting a priority. Both the New York Police Department (NYPD) and the Los Angeles Police Department (LAPD) have created specialized anti-piracy units, the Trademark Infringement Unit at NYPD and the Anti-Piracy Unit at LAPD.[18] These units seek to target the large manufacturers and distributors rather than street vendors.

Since 1994, the NYPD has operated the special Trademark Infringement Unit (TIU) within its Organized Crime Investigation Unit and is one of the few units in the country that exclusively works trademark cases. At the time of the TIU's inception, reproduction of music and movies was a time-consuming task, and the quality of the reproductions was poor, so the unit focused primarily on sales of T-shirts bearing licensed logos and characters. This earned the unit the title "the T-shirt squad." Today the TIU works with numerous companies and their trade associations to identify sources of counterfeit products, such as DVDs, fashion, and auto parts, as well as to locate the marketplaces in which those products are sold. The TIU is housed in the same division as the NYPD's organized-crime investigations, because of the belief that extensive criminal networks lie behind the counterfeiting operations. In 2006, the NYPD shut down 75 counterfeiting establishments, made 600 felony arrests, and gave out 6,000 court summonses.

The LAPD's Anti-Piracy Unit was established in 2004. It focuses on trademark crimes involving mid-level distribution of trademarked goods and the manufacturing of counterfeit products. The unit is housed within the LAPD's central vice division. In addition to building cases against middle- to large-scale counterfeiting operations, the unit is responsible for training the rest of the police force on counterfeiting issues, usually through roll calls at local stations, but also

---

[18] This section relies heavily on interviews with officers in the two departments.

through more-formal courses, such as one of the lessons in the LAPD's five-day vice school.

Along with many other state and local agencies, including the Los Angeles County Sheriff's office and the District Attorney's office, the LAPD helped form the Los Angeles Anti-Piracy Task Force, which is the clearinghouse for regional anti-piracy efforts. At the start of the 2007 holiday shopping season, this task force raided Santee Alley, a widely known local place where pirated movies and music are sold, as well as cheap knock-offs of popular fashion.[19] The operation, called "Operation Knockout," put 140 officers into Santee Alley on one day; the officers confiscated counterfeit goods with a street value of $8 million and arrested 26 suspects on trademark counterfeiting charges.

At the NYPD and the LAPD, all patrol officers are trained to identify suspected trademark counterfeiting. The NYPD is widely known for its stop, question, and frisk approach to crime control in New York City. It is NYPD policy that officers who observe suspicious behavior that is indicative of pirated DVD sales are to stop and question the individuals involved and immediately refer the case to the TIU.

The LAPD indicated that officers have discretion as to whether they should investigate suspicious activity that is consistent with sales of pirated materials. This regulation is partly due to the fact that Los Angeles has only about half as many officers per capita as New York City, and therefore the officers are less able to spend time on lower-priority investigations such as street peddling of counterfeit goods.

Eradicating Space for Crime

Street busts have the additional benefit of improving public safety in the communities in which they occur by removing a physical protected space for more serious crimes. Both the NYPD and the LAPD indicated that the main problem with sales of pirated material is that, as a cash-based business, it creates an easy target for traditional crimes; all cash businesses, legal and illegal, are exposed to these threats. Extor-

---

[19] Andrew Blankstein and Susannah Rosenblatt, "Santee Alley fakes seized in raid," *Los Angeles Times,* December 1, 2007.

tion of vendors by street gangs, for example, is hardly uncommon in Los Angeles.[20]

Robbery and extortion victims involved in illegal sales of pirated goods are unlikely to report those incidents to the police. Criminals looking for good targets take advantage of counterfeiters' reticence to involve law enforcement, and this exposes all those involved—the vendors, customers, and passersby—to the risk of violence. In 2005, a tourist in New York was shot during a robbery of a vendor of counterfeit goods.[21] In such current circumstances, the greatest disincentive to DVD piracy may be extortion and violence carried out by competing DVD pirates or other criminals.

This is an argument for one set of public safety benefits from increased law enforcement efforts. Situational crime-prevention theory suggests that a key strategy for disrupting crime is that of removing opportunities for criminal activity.[22] This theory provides the motivation for communities to increase street lighting, cities to lock down abandoned structures, and businesses to supplement local law enforcement with private security. All of these decrease the access to and attractiveness of certain places for criminal activity. Stepped-up enforcement against counterfeit vending operations removes a particularly appealing environment for criminal activity.

Leveraging Piracy for Criminal Intelligence

A critical issue at the intersection of intelligence and law enforcement deserves further exploration: How might the piracy issue be leveraged for broader law enforcement and security purposes? DVD piracy is not a very interesting crime for law enforcement unless it is also linked with

---

[20] Ari B. Bloomekatz, "Sad price of gang 'rent': A street vendor who owed was the target, but a baby died. The LAPD cracks down," *Los Angeles Times,* October 7, 2007, p. B1.

[21] Nicholas Confessore, "No-Name, brand-name or phony: It's all here," *New York Times,* October 9, 2006.

[22] Ronald V. Clarke, "Situational Crime Prevention: Its Theoretical Basis and Practical Scope," in Michael H. Tonry and Norval Morris (eds.), *Crime and Justice: An Annual Review of Research,* Vol. 4, Chicago, IL: University of Chicago Press, 1983, pp. 225–256.

more "serious" crimes, such as human trafficking and gun smuggling. Dorm-room pirates may be an economic problem for the industry, and perhaps a moral question mark for society, but they are not a public safety problem. The cases and analysis presented in Chapters Four and Five establish that film piracy is nested with other crimes, but can following up on piracy leads provide intelligence about more-serious criminal activity? This issue is important enough to merit assessing in more detail.

In one case, that of Lotus Trading Company in Britain, the discovery of piracy did lead directly to uncovering more-serious crimes. In most of the others, evidence of piracy was found in the course of investigating more serious crimes, such as human smuggling. Two police departments that do work hard on counterfeiting, the NYPD and the LAPD, raise the issue of how and to what extent those efforts can provide intelligence about dangerous individuals or leads for tackling organized-crime networks.

These units have explored using DVD piracy investigations or arrests as leverage to crack down on wider criminal activities. One strategy was to use DVD vending as a parallel to turnstile jumping or marijuana possession. To address increasing crime rates in the 1990s, the NYPD began stopping individuals for minor offenses such as jumping transit turnstiles, finding that many of these individuals were involved in more-serious crimes, had outstanding warrants, and/ or carried weapons. Focusing on a seemingly victimless crime such as turnstile-jumping gave police a legal pretext on which to detain individuals for further investigation.

The LAPD reported to us that the majority of DVDs sold on the street are burned DVDs, have laser-printed covers, and come in 5mm cases (rather than the standard 10mm)—all indicative of home-based operations rather than criminal networks. Street peddlers arrested on trademark counterfeiting charges often have a criminal history, but that history consists almost exclusively of prior counterfeiting arrests. This is not always the case, however, as the LAPD noted a few cases in which arrests of vendors resulted in the recovery of illegal firearms or narcotics. The frequency of such cases appeared to be increasing as street gangs increasingly become involved in counterfeiting and piracy.

Officers in both departments interview arrestees to obtain information about their operations. However, another of the effects of the relatively minor penalties for piracy offenses, compared with, for instance, penalties for crimes involving drugs, is that suspects arrested on piracy offenses have little incentive to cooperate in taking an investigation to other levels or other crimes. As a result, NYPD officials indicated, piracy busts rarely result in larger busts. An LAPD officer noted that DVD street vendors who are approached are likely to simply run away, abandoning their pirated DVD collection. Since the cost of DVD production is minimal, their greatest financial loss is the abandoned folding table and duffle bag.

The FBI-led Joint Terrorism Task Forces (JTTFs) have had some success in pursuing counterfeiting and terrorist financing investigations. Because the JTTFs focus only on the most serious counterfeiting cases (those that are linked with terrorism), and in virtue of their unique partnership of federal and local agencies, it is worth considering how this structure might be a model of innovation in responding to the links between organized crime, terrorism, and film piracy.

Through the JTTFs, intelligence authorities collaborate with state and local agencies and an array of federal agencies to prevent future terrorist attacks and share intelligence. The first JTTF was established in New York City in 1980, and after September 11, 2001, JTTFs tripled in number; there are more than 100 today,[23] each staffed with an average of 40 to 50 people. Larger task forces, such as those in New York, can have as many as 550 agents.[24] Other specialized experts also join the JTTFs—in particular, members seconded from Immigration and Customs Enforcement (ICE), the lead U.S. federal agency that handles

---

[23] K. Jack Riley, Gregory F. Treverton, Jeremy M. Wilson, and Lois M. Davis, *State and Local Intelligence in the War on Terrorism*, Santa Monica, CA: RAND Corporation, MG-394-RC, 2005, p. 3. Available at http://www.rand.org/pubs/monographs/MG394/ (as of September 22, 2008).

[24] U.S. Department of Justice, Federal Bureau of Investigation, *Report to the National Commission on Terrorist Attacks upon the United States: The FBI's Counterterrorism Program Since September 2001*, Submitted April 14, 2004. Available at http://www.fbi.gov/publications/commission/9-11commissionrep.pdf (as of August 1, 2008).

piracy, counterfeiting, and smuggling investigations. In 2003, the FBI launched a new program to identify and train terrorist financing coordinators to be located within each JTTF.[25] The pairing of anti-counterfeiting and financial-crimes investigators has already yielded several successful operations that have dismantled terrorist financing networks that drew profits from counterfeiting businesses (among other illicit activities such as narcotics trafficking).

Recent cases include the Detroit JTTF's investigation of Karim Hassan Nasser and 18 other targets for funneling to Hezbollah money raised from the proceeds of contraband cigarettes, counterfeit Zig Zag rolling papers, and counterfeit Viagra. Nasser and eight others were arrested on March 29, 2006, when the indictment was unsealed.[26] The Los Angeles JTTF spearheaded a two-year investigation that led to the arrest of Ali Khalil Elreda and 11 other targets. An indictment unsealed in November 2007 revealed that the JTTF seized 30 kilograms of cocaine and hundreds of thousands of dollars worth of counterfeit clothing from Elreda and his associates.[27] Elreda and his cohorts are also said to be under investigation for transferring proceeds from this enterprise to a Lebanese terrorist organization.[28]

The role of the JTTFs could be enhanced by including more ICE agents with direct knowledge of IPR criminal investigations and promoting an expanded partnership between ICE agents and local law enforcement. Because of the low priority assigned to IPR cases by local

---

[25] U.S. Department of Justice, Office of the Inspector General Audit Division, *The Federal Bureau of Investigation's Efforts to Improve the Sharing of Intelligence and Other Information*, Audit Report 04-10, December 2003. Available at http://www.usdoj.gov/oig/reports/FBI/a0410/final.pdf (as of August 1, 2008).

[26] U.S. Department of Justice, "Nineteen Charged with Racketeering to Support Terrorist Organization," press release, March 29, 2006. Available at http://detroit.fbi.gov/dojpressrel/pressrel06/de032906a.htm (as of August 1, 2008).

[27] U.S. Department of Justice, "Operation Bell Bottoms Targets Counterfeiting, Narcotics Operation in Los Angeles-Area Clothing Stores," press release, November 6, 2007. Available at http://losangeles.fbi.gov/dojpressrel/pressrel07/la110607busa.htm (as of August 1, 2008).

[28] Terrorism allegations were confirmed by confidential interviews. Also see similar claims by knowledgeable sources in James Gordon Meek, "Busted Los Angeles drug ring had ties to Hezbollah," *Daily News Washington Bureau*, November 21, 2007.

police agencies and the turf battles among them, ICE agents have complained that they often learn about seizures too late to collect evidence of possible links to terrorism or organized crime.

More street-level enforcement can produce the benefit of eradicating criminal space, but it alone will not produce more than low-level arrests. It will take a strategy, one including higher penalties for piracy—as discussed in the following chapter—to make enforcement against piracy fruitful in uncovering connections to the organized crime with which it is nested.

Developing that strategy will require the kind of change in attitudes that occurred in Hong Kong when connections with more-visceral safety concerns became manifest through investigations and arrests—such as a connection to human or drug smuggling. The case studies presented in this report make clear that the connections between counterfeiting and organized crime exist, yet often it takes deeper investigations to uncover the links back to serious crime and terrorism. Investigations of those connections should be driven by an intelligence-centered agenda: How are the various targets connected? Who is in charge? Who supplies the group? Law enforcement authorities and intelligence officials must be given the tools they need to explore and expose these connections in order to learn more about how organized-crime syndicates and terrorist groups operate, so that they can be disrupted.

CHAPTER EIGHT

The Way Forward

The obstacles to combating intellectual-property piracy are formidable. Against them, what can be done? And what should be done? This chapter begins with efforts to reduce demand for pirated goods and with international law and IPR regimes. The latter offer a way of bringing developing countries such as China into the fold as they, too, begin to have intellectual property to protect. But both decreasing supply and reducing demand of pirated goods take time. The gap between signing treaties and implementing them on the ground will remain frustratingly large. Accordingly, this chapter offers a number of recommendations aimed at getting piracy and other counterfeiting the attention they deserve given the extent of organized crime's involvement and the nascent links to terrorism. While finding additional resources will be hard, finding new, smarter ways of deploying resources will be imperative.

Changing the Face of Demand

Most of this report has addressed the *supply* side; it has focused on the criminals or terrorists, their operations, and their profits. Yet counterfeiting is a complicit crime; without demand there would be no supply. What about efforts to reduce demand? Italy, for instance, has criminalized demand by making it illegal to buy counterfeit products. Trying to cut prices to compete with counterfeiters is probably a losing strategy, because making and marketing a motion picture is an expensive enterprise, and given the pirates' enormous profit margins, the price

cuts in legal DVDs would have to be very large indeed in many countries to make much difference. The counterfeiters would win that "race
to the bottom."

However, IPR advocates might work with trade and commerce
officials to encourage the continual opening of markets, like China's,
to allow more films to be released in foreign theaters. Indeed, films are
increasingly being released simultaneously in different markets. However, making DVDs available simultaneously with theatrical releases
is more problematic, both because of the economics of studios and
exhibitors and because a gap is mandated by law in some countries.

Another approach would be to begin to change the face of demand
based on the message of this report. Buying pirated films may support
organized crime and the range of crimes, including violent crimes, in
which those groups engage. In some instances, organized crime may
provide funding for terrorist groups. Surveys suggest that while most
people who acquire illegal copies of films know that what they did is
illegal, they regard their act as a relatively innocent white crime.[1]

Surveys also suggest that the attitudes of pirates might change if
they knew their actions were supporting organized crime and terrorism. In one survey, 74 percent of pirates under the age of 25 and 69
percent of those over 25 said they would be "less likely" to engage in
piracy if they were concerned that piracy was tied to criminal activities
and terrorism. Simple reminders of illegality can help as well, for similar percentages of pirates said they would be "less likely" to engage in
piracy if they received warnings of possible prosecution. For instance,
during the 2007 holiday season, the British government posted warnings for consumers about counterfeit goods, including DVDs and CDs,
along with tips for recognizing them.

More recently, the British intellectual-property trust employed a
"Knock Off Nigel" campaign aimed at teenagers, portraying piracy
as "un-cool." When the campaign began, in May 2007, 36 percent of
British teenagers surveyed said they considered unauthorized downloading and file sharing a "crime"; by December, the proportion had

---

[1] The most extensive study is one that was done for the MPA. The following results are from
it.

increased to 56 percent.[2] This change in perception manifested itself in behavior, as the number of British consumers who admitted buying illegal DVDs dropped from 8 percent to 6 percent, and the number who admitted borrowing them dropped from 15 percent to 11 percent over the same period.[3] This approach to reducing demand is no doubt more promising in countries such as the United States and Britain, where economic factors drive piracy less and concern about terrorism is more salient.

Approaches to Mitigating Film Piracy: Treaty Regimes

Another way forward is to build on international law, IPR regimes in particular. States with IPR to protect have negotiated international instruments as far back as the Paris Convention for the Protection of Industrial Property (1883) and the Berne Convention for the Protection of Literary and Artistic Works (1886). With the development of knowledge-based economies and low-cost media, countries with industries whose IPR was deemed at risk pursued additional protections through a web of treaties.

Of all the treaties, however, the WTO's Agreement on Trade-Related Aspects of Intellectual Property Rights Agreement (TRIPS) is probably both the strongest and most relevant, given the WTO's wide membership and its dispute-resolution mechanism.[4] The WTO does, however, suffer from an image that it protects rich companies at the expense of poor countries, since it requires member states to provide minimum legal protections and remedies for various types of IPR enforcement.

---

[2] "Campaign Changes Views on Piracy," *Screen Digest*, March 2008 Newsletter, p. 73.

[3] Ibid.

[4] The WTO had 151 members as of July 27, 2007, whereas the WIPO Copyright Treaty has only 64 (27 of which have not entered it into force). See *List of Contracting Parties to WIPO*, available at http://www.wipo.int/treaties/en/ShowResults.jsp?lang=en&treaty_id=16 (as of December 17, 2007); *List of WTO Members and Observers*, available at http://www.wto.org/english/thewto_e/whatis_e/tif_e/org6_e.htm (as of December 17, 2007).

TRIPS is different from the usual focus on *civil-law* protections of IPR in international agreements. Those protections encourage member states to create civil laws, rights, and remedies that harmonize with other signing states, along with the necessary administrative and due process framework (such as registry offices) to enforce those rights, and non-discrimination rules to allow foreign IPR owners to register and protect their IPR locally. In contrast, TRIPS explicitly requires states to use *criminal laws* to protect IPR. Specifically, it requires criminal procedures and penalties—including imprisonment, fines, and forfeitures—to deter willful trademark counterfeiting and copyright piracy on a commercial scale.[5]

How effective treaty regimes can be for dealing with counterfeiting in general, and film piracy in particular, is not yet clear. The gap between signing and implementing policies to satisfy TRIPS is a yawning one for many countries; strong intentions at the top of government are still frustrated by uneven implementation at the local level. Effective enforcement of TRIPS requires a legal structure and a judiciary that understands and values IPR, a police force that gives priority to IPR-related investigations, resources to support operations that are becoming increasingly technologically advanced as pirates utilize new technology, and most important, anti-corruption measures at the local and regional level. Only then can harmonizing criminal law allow the usual tools of international cooperation—mutual legal assistance and extradition treaties—to come into play. And even when these processes work, they are slow, for they depend on the cooperation of multiple bureaucracies in many countries.

A Broader Agenda for Action

Clearly, better enforcement of IPR laws is all to the good. And as countries such as China come to recognize that the IP laws are good for

---

[5] TRIPS Article 61. Criminal penalties for IPR infringement are a relatively late and infrequent addition to IPR protections. Despite the fact that IPR infringement is intrinsically "theft," civil rather than criminal remedies are the norm. The traditional IPR enforcement mechanism is the private lawsuit brought by the owner of intellectual property rights against the alleged infringer of the right(s). This reveals a reinforced perception of IP theft as a victimless crime.

them too, enforcement will improve. However, for many countries, incentives will long remain weak and capability even weaker. What, then, might constitute a broader agenda for action? If the bad guys— organized crime—have a portfolio of criminal activities, the good guys—policymakers, law enforcement, and industry—need a portfolio of responses.

Five factors bear on the effectiveness of IPR policies: strong government and political will, good legislation, fair and consistent enforcement, deterrent sentencing, and willingness to experiment with innovative solutions. Governments that are serious about combating piracy need, first, to diagnose their own shortcomings in light of these five factors, then they must frame initiatives to address those shortcomings.

Strong Government and Political Will

No government can mount a comprehensive strategy against counterfeiting or piracy without first being willing to do so. Willingness manifests itself in many forms. Some examples are:

- Providing more resources. Governments, both national and local, will make their own decisions about how much to spend in the fight against counterfeiting or piracy. But the case for more is stronger the more clearly the link between counterfeiting and organized crime is understood to be, and stronger still given the evidence of funding terrorism. Australia, for instance, has recently authorized $12 million to fight organized crime linked to intellectual-property piracy.
- Creating executive-level positions that include responsibility for IPR protection and economic growth. Within five months of winning the presidency, France's Nicholas Sarkozy appointed Finance Minister Dennis Olivennes to negotiate a landmark agreement to establish an independent government body to implement an "Internet service provider graduated response" program to decrease online piracy. In the United States, the Office of the U.S. Attorney General includes an Intellectual Property Task Force. These types of high-level political appointments help focus political will

to accomplish specific objectives and usually result in a dramatic advance in IPR policy.

- Funding "intellectual-property attachés" to be stationed at U.S. (and perhaps other nations') embassies in major commercial markets—such as Britain, Spain, Germany, and Japan—to train local law enforcement on techniques for developing cases against organized networks of pirates, sharing intelligence, and coordinating government resources against intellectual-property crime.

- Placing organized crime and piracy on the agenda of influential international government and business gatherings such as the G-8 and the Davos Economic Summit.

- Holding periodic legislative hearings or other high-visibility government-driven public-awareness campaigns.

- Increasing specialized enforcement training. Policing organizations must receive adequate training and funding in order to understand the link between organized crime and IPR as well as to carry out their mandates effectively. Various countries have linked piracy with economic-crime enforcement units such as Italy's Guardia di Finanzia and Britain's Trade and Standards, which enforces the Proceeds of Crime Act. These "IPR police" may be more effective than regular officers in tracing information related to serious crimes.

- Improving intelligence-sharing between intelligence services (which track terrorists) and law enforcement authorities (who investigate instances of counterfeiting and criminal networks), both within countries and, where feasible, between countries.

- Permitting customs authorities to provide rights holders and appropriate authorities with information on the importers and exporters of seemingly counterfeit goods, as well as information about the countries of origin of such goods.

Good Legislation

The starting point for any improved strategy has to be the recognition that large-scale counterfeiting is organized crime—in its methods, its profitability, and its links to groups that commit other crimes. Legislative provisions should establish penalties for all the phases linked to counterfeiting, from production to sales, without distinguishing between activities focusing on the exporting, transit, or importing phases of non-original goods. Activities linked to the commission of the crime, such as the storage of goods or the supply of raw materials, should also be given consideration. Effective organized-crime legislation comprises a few key elements that give law enforcement a reasonable chance to take on hardened organized-crime syndicates involved in counterfeiting and piracy:

- Expanding the definition of organized-crime statutes to include commercial-scale piracy and counterfeiting tied with other criminal activity. Countries that have begun to incorporate copyright provisions in their organized-crime and money-laundering statutes include India (1999 Maharashtra Control of Organized Crime Act); Japan (1999 Law Concerning Punishment of Organized Crime, Law No. 136); Hong Kong (2000 Organized and Serious Crime Ordinance (Cap 455)); Malaysia (2001 Anti-Money Laundering Act); Korea (2001 Anti-Money Laundering Act); and the Philippines (2001 Republic Act No. 9160, Anti-Money Laundering Act).
- Being more proactive by giving investigators greater authority to conduct surveillance and obtain search warrants, on the model of Hong Kong.
- Reviewing the "knowledge" or *mens rea* requirement for federal IPC prosecutions. At present, investigations often are stymied when factory owners claim ignorance of counterfeiting occurring at their facilities.[6]

Fair and Consistent Enforcement

- Establishing protocols for investigations, with training to match. Street busts are just that unless they begin to unravel the chain of organization. The protocols would be guidelines for pursuing

---

[6] Under the current U.S. Criminal Code (18 U.S.C. § 2318, 2319, 2319b), prosecutors need to prove that the defendant "knowingly" committed or assisted in a criminal copyright infringement.

investigations in greater depth, and especially for trying to trace back the production and distribution chain for the counterfeit goods. A particular challenge for customs inspectors, given the increasing quality of the counterfeit goods and their packaging, is distinguishing the counterfeits from legally produced goods.

- Processing cases efficiently. Organized-crime cases must be handled quickly and given priority by the judiciary, lest backlogs delay proceedings and hamper prosecutors' abilities to secure testimony before informants are intimidated.

- Enhancing international cooperation. Organized-crime groups know no political boundaries and work across jurisdictions, precisely to frustrate investigative efforts. IPR enforcement authorities must leverage international agencies such as Interpol and the WCO to remain as agile as the criminals they are tracking.

Deterrent Sentencing

The current relatively light penalties for counterfeiting do not serve as much of a deterrent, nor do they provide much incentive for those arrested to cooperate in turning a street bust into a deeper investigation of organized crime. In fact, when weak sentences that amount to "slaps on the wrist" are compared with big potential profits, the balance is easily tipped in favor of the money.

In the words of a recent UN report: "Even in the case of 'street' counterfeiting—visible every day in numerous cities and mostly involving CDs or DVDs or luxury goods—it is highly probable that organized criminal groups are involved; the final seller is often a victim her/himself of the phenomenon, exploited and forced to sell counterfeit products by criminal gangs."[7] Truly deterrent criminal penalties, not the administrative sanctions that are the norm in many places, are thus imperative. In many cases, small fines are simply a cost of doing business factored into gaping profit margins.

---

[7] *Counterfeiting: A Global Spread, A Global Threat,* Report of the Anti-Human Trafficking and Emerging Crimes Unit of the United Nations Interregional Crime and Justice Research Institute (UNICRI), Turin, Italy, December 2007, p. 128.

There is always a risk, one very apparent in narcotics cases, that harsh penalties will afflict the foot soldiers, while the higher-ups within organized criminal syndicates remain protected. But those street peddlers who are themselves victims should be relatively easy to sort out, and harsher penalties are critical to strategies of both deterrence and deeper investigation.

The following additional recommendations would strengthen deterrent prosecution:

- Fight key piracy cases in the organized-crime or money-laundering divisions of the prosecutor's office. Cases that are handled in the general prosecutorial divisions often receive less priority than more-violent crimes and may, as well, focus on the "easy" targets (e.g., the peddlers), not the organized-crime leaders.
- Work to reduce the money in IPR crime. That could mean using Asset Recovery/Proceeds of Crime legislation to fight intellectual-property-crime cases with organized-crime involvement. In the United States, the effort could include, for instance, using FinCEN (the Treasury Department's Financial Crimes Enforcement Network) and other Treasury and Justice Department financial-crimes experts to follow the money trail, along with stronger application of money-laundering statutes, though these government agencies are hard pressed to accomplish their current mandates.
- Include movie piracy as a priority offense within federal, state, and local anti-gang strategies.

Willingness to Experiment with Innovative Solutions

A government's willingness to be innovative in its attempts to curb counterfeit theft should not be underestimated. Indeed, it will be only through innovative solutions that this unique crime can be reduced. Innovative solutions might include:

- Considering making piracy, especially large-scale piracy, an extraditable offense in bilateral and multilateral treaties.

- Amending customs and immigration forms to include language prohibiting the importation of counterfeit goods. The absence of a specifically worded prohibition may cause some travelers to question whether piracy or counterfeiting is considered "as bad" as the importation of agriculture, plants, fruits, and meats, prohibition of which is currently enumerated.
- Identifying and holding responsible landlords/owners of buildings located in black markets (such as Tepito in Mexico City) for the illegal pirate trade their tenants conduct. Authorities could also shut down flea markets that continue to sell counterfeit goods despite orders to cease and desist.
- Enlisting the support of the financial community, online-payment processors, and digital-payment facilitators. Banks should be engaged to help authorities spot piracy syndicates' money-laundering tactics and ultimately to limit the financial services available to beneficiaries of copyright infringement. Payment processors (Visa/MasterCard) and search engines (Google, Yahoo!) provide filters against child porn. It is worth exploring whether payment processors could be facilitating financial transactions with pirate websites, especially hard-goods websites, to the benefit of organized crime. More broadly, it is worth assessing the role the Internet plays in the sale and distribution of counterfeits, including hard goods.
- Improving standards for transportation documents. Counterfeiting frequently is associated with forged transportation documents—for instance, under-invoicing, which also facilitates laundering the proceeds of the crime. Industry itself has moved to make its products more secure by applying bar codes or holograms, but the same techniques have not yet been applied to transportation documents.
- Working with the World Bank. Two decades ago, it would have been regarded as intervention for the World Bank to point to corruption in any given nation. Now, fighting corruption and improving governance are major thrusts of the Bank's activity. The Bank could make reducing piracy an indicator of a borrower's suitability for continued lending.

- Increasing education concerning IPR generally. Education is critical to combating intellectual-property theft, because many students and adults do not know what intellectual-property theft is, nor are they informed about resultant consequences.

There is no doubt that organized crime is involved in piracy, but additional research could assess the share of pirated movies that are linked to organized crime or which features of transactions (for instance, the form of the media or sale location) are good predictors of organized crime's involvement. Producers have more to gain than to lose from better information. For their part, national authorities could systematically provide data on, for instance, the number of seizures at borders, what is seized, where the goods came from, concealment methods used, types of forged documents, criminal organizations suspected, areas most affected, and outcomes of any enforcement action.

The point is that only with better information will government officials, law enforcement authorities, and private industry around the world respond by devoting more resources to combating counterfeiting of all types, including film piracy, thus exposing the connections to organized crime and ultimately choking off a growing revenue stream for criminal enterprises and for terrorism.

Bibliography

2007 Corruption Perceptions Index, Transparency International. Available at http://www.transparency.org/policy_research/surveys_indices/cpi/2007 (as of September 29, 2008).

Albright, David, *Al Qaeda's Nuclear Program: Through the Window of Seized Documents*, Policy Forum Online Special Forum 47, November 6, 2002. Available at http://www.nautilus.org/fora/Special-Policy-Forum/47_Albright.html (as of September 12, 2008).

Arena, Michael P., "Hizballah's Global Criminal Operations," *Global Crime*, Vol. 7, No. 3-4, August–November 2006.

Billingslea, William, "Illicit Cigarette Trafficking and the Funding of Terrorism," *The Police Chief*, February 2004, pp. 49–54.

Bratton, William F., "The Mutation of the Illegal Trade Market," *The Police Chief*, May 2007.

Broussard, Phillippe, "Dangerous Fakes," *World Press Review*, Vol. 44, No. 1, January 1999.

Canadian Centre for Intelligence and Security Studies, The Norman Patterson School of International Affairs, Carleton University, *Actual and Potential Links Between Terrorism and Criminality*, Volume 2006-5, Integrated Threat Assessment Centre, ITAC Trends in Terrorism Series, Vol. 5, No. 4, 2006.

Chu, Yi Kong, "Hong Kong Triads after 1997," *Trends in Organized Crime*, Vol. 8, No. 3, March 2005, pp. 5–12.

Clarke, Ronald V., "Situational Crime Prevention: Its Theoretical Basis and Practical Scope," in Michael H. Tonry and Norval Morris (eds.), *Crime and Justice: An Annual Review of Research*, Vol. 4, Chicago, IL: University of Chicago Press, 1983, pp. 225–256.

Code of Federal Regulations, 28 C.F.R. Section 0.85.

Counterfeiting: A Global Spread, A Global Threat, Report of the Anti-Human Trafficking and Emerging Crimes Unit of the United Nations Interregional Crime and Justice Research Institute (UNICRI), Turin, Italy, December 2007.

Cragin, Kim, and Sara Daley, *Assessing the Dynamic Terrorist Threat*, Santa Monica, CA: RAND Corporation, RB-121-AF, 2004. Available at http://www.rand.org/pubs/research_briefs/RB121/ (as of September 24, 2008).

Crime Prevention and Criminal Justice: Report of the Ad Hoc Committee on the Elaboration of a Convention Against Transnational Organized Crime on the Work of Its First to Eleventh Sessions, United Nations General Assembly, November 2, 2000, UNA/55/383. Available at http://www.uncjin.org/Documents/Conventions/dcatoc/final_documents/383e.pdf (as of September 12, 2008).

Cunan, Anne L., "U.S. and International Responses," in Jeanne K. Giraldo and Harold A. Trinkunas (eds.), *Terrorism Financing and State Responses: A Comparative Perspective*, Stanford, CA: Stanford University Press, 2007.

Curtis, Glenn E., et al., *Transnational Activities of Chinese Crime Organizations*, Washington, D.C.: Congressional Research Service, April 2003.

Daffarra, Luciano, report on Camorra Piracy for MPA, November 29, 2006.

Daly, John C.K., "The Latin Connection," *Terrorism Monitor*, Vol. 1, Issue 3, October 10, 2003. Available at http://jamestown.org/publications_details.php?volume_id=391&issue_id=2877&article_id=23407 (as of September 28, 2008).

Dishman, Chris, "The Leaderless Nexus: When Crime and Terror Converge," *Studies in Conflict & Terrorism*, Vol. 28, No. 3, 2005.

———, "Terrorism, Crime, and Transformation," *Studies in Conflict & Terrorism*, Vol. 24, No. 1, 2001.

Evans, Richard, "Organised crime and terrorist financing in Northern Ireland," *Jane's Intelligence Review*, August 9, 2002.

Felson, Marcus, *Crime and Everyday Life: Insight and Implications for Society*, Thousand Oaks, CA: Pine Forge Press, 1994.

Finckenauer, James O., and Ko-lin Chin, *Asian Transnational Organized Crime*, U.S. Department of Justice, Office of Justice Programs, National Institute of Justice Special Report, January 2007.

Finckenauer, James O., and Yuri A. Voronin, *The Threat of Russian Organized Crime*, Washington, D.C.: National Institute of Justice, June 2001. Available at http://www.ncjrs.gov/pdffiles1/nij/187085.pdf (as of September 24, 2008).

Galeotti, Mark, "Japanese yakuza consolidation risks strife in Tokyo," *Jane's Intelligence Review*, November 1, 2005.

————, "Yakuza splits into 'white-collar' and violent crime," *Jane's Intelligence Review*, June 1, 2001.

————, "Chinese crime's global reach," *Jane's Intelligence Review*, November 1, 2000.

Giraldo, Jeanne K., and Harold A. Trinkunas, "The Political Economy of Terrorist Financing," in Jeanne K. Giraldo and Harold A. Trinkunas (eds.), *Terrorism Financing and State Responses: A Comparative Perspective*, Stanford, CA: Stanford University Press, 2007.

Goulka, Jeremiah, and Stephen Nelleman, "Drugged Law Enforcement: The Influence of Drug Trafficking on Human Rights and the Rule of Law in Mexico," in William Cartwright (ed.), *Mexico: Facing the Challenges of Human Rights and Crime*, Ardsley, NY: Transnational Publishers, 1999, pp. 23–39.

Greenberg, Maurice R., et al., *Terrorist Financing: Report of an Independent Task Force Sponsored by the Council on Foreign Relations*, New York: Council on Foreign Relations, November 25, 2002.

Hamm, Mark S., *Crimes Committed by Terrorist Groups: Theory, Research, and Prevention*, Washington, D.C.: U.S. Department of Justice, Office of Justice Programs, June 1, 2005. Available at http://www.ncjrs.gov/pdffiles1/nij/grants/211203.pdf (as of September 12, 2008).

Harmon, Christopher C., *Terrorism Today*, London and Portland, OR: Frank Cass, 2000.

Harper, T. N., *The End of Empire and the Making of Malaya*, Cambridge, UK: Cambridge University Press, 2001.

Harmon, Christopher C., *Terrorism Today*, London and Portland, OR: Frank Cass, 2000.

Helfand, Neil S., *Asian Organized Crime and Terrorist Activity in Canada, 1999-2002*, Washington, D.C.: Library of Congress, Federal Research Division, July 2003. Available at http://www.loc.gov/rr/frd/pdf-files/AsianOrgCrime_Canada.pdf (as of September 28, 2008).

Hill, John, and Ann Rogers, "Triad societies seek increased opportunities as China opens up," *Jane's Intelligence Review*, January 1, 2003.

Hill, Peter, "The Changing Face of the Yakuza," *Global Crime*, Vol. 6, No. 1, February 2004.

————, "Heisei Yakuza: Burst Bubble and Botaiho" *Social Science Japan Journal*, Vol. 6, No. 1, 2003.

Hoffman, Bruce, *Inside Terrorism*, New York: Columbia University Press, 1998.

Horgan, John, and Max Taylor, "Playing the 'Green Card'—Financing the Provisional IRA: Part 1," *Terrorism and Political Violence*, Vol. 11, No. 2, Summer 1999, pp. 1–38.

Hudson, Rex, *Terrorist and Organized Crime Groups in the Tri-Border Area (TBA) of South America*, Washington, D.C.: Federal Research Division, Library of Congress, July 2003.

Hunter, Tom, "Russia's mafiyas: The new revolution," *Jane's Intelligence Review*, June 1997.

Hutchinson, Steven, and Pat O'Malley, "A Crime-Terror Nexus? Thinking on Some of the Links between Terrorism and Criminality," *Studies in Conflict & Terrorism*, Vol. 30, No. 12, 2007, pp. 7–8.

Independent Monitoring Commission of Northern Ireland. Available at http://www.independentmonitoringcommission.org/index.cfm (as of September 24, 2008).

———, *Seventeenth Report of the Independent Monitoring Commission*, November 2007, paragraphs 2.15 and 2.16. Available at http://www.independentmonitoringcommission.org/documents/uploads/17th_IMC.pdf (as of September 24, 2008).

———, *First Report of the Independent Monitoring Commission*, April 2004, paragraph 6.13. Available at http://www.independentmonitoringcommission.org/documents/uploads/First%20Report.doc (as of September 24, 2008).

International Intellectual Property Alliance, *Special 301 Report*, 2007, p. 10. Available at http://www.iipa.com/2007_SPEC301_TOC.htm (as of September 28, 2008).

———, *Special 201 Report: Malaysia*, 2005. Available at http://www.iipa.com/rbc/2005/2005SPEC301MALAYSIArev.pdf (as of August 13, 2008).

Jackson, Brian A., John C. Baker, Peter Chalk, Kim Cragin, John V. Parachini, and Horacio R. Trujillo, *Aptitude for Destruction: Volume 1, Organizational Learning in Terrorist Groups and Its Implications for Combating Terrorism*, Santa Monica, CA: RAND Corporation, MG-331-NIJ, 2005. Available at http://www.rand.org/pubs/monographs/MG331/ (as of September 24, 2008).

Jackson, Brian A., Peter Chalk, Kim Cragin, Bruce Newsome, John V. Parachini, William Rosenau, Erin M. Simpson, Melanie Sisson, and Donald Temple,

Breaching the Fortress Wall: Understanding Terrorist Efforts to Overcome Defensive Technologies, Santa Monica, CA: RAND Corporation, MG-481-DHS, 2007. Available at http://www.rand.org/pubs/monographs/MG481/ (as of September 24, 2008).

Jamieson, Alison, "Italy's gangs change their tactics," *Jane's Intelligence Review*, November 21, 2001.

Kaplan, David E., and Alec Dubro, *Yakuza: Japan's Criminal Underworld*, Berkeley, CA: University of California Press, 2003.

King, Gilbert, *The Most Dangerous Man in the World: Dawood Ibrahim: Billionaire Gangster, Protector of Osama Bin Laden, Nuclear Black Market Entrepreneur, Islamic Extremist, and Global Terrorist*, New York: Chamberlain Bros., 2004.

Knight, Helen, "Fighting the Fakers," *The Engineer*, April 26, 2002.

Levitt, Matthew, "Hezbollah Finances: Funding the Party of God," in Jeanne K. Giraldo and Harold A. Trinkunas (eds.), *Terrorism Financing and State Responses: A Comparative Perspective*, Stanford, CA: Stanford University Press, 2007.

Levitt, Matthew, and David Schenker, "Who Was Imad Mughniyeh?" *Policywatch #1340*, Washington Institute for Near East Policy, February 14, 2008. Available at http://www.washingtoninstitute.org/templateC05.php?CID=2716 (as of September 28, 2008).

Liddick, Don, and Ronald R. Liddick, *The Global Underworld: Transnational Crime and the United States*, Westport, CT: Greenwood Publishing Group, 2004.

Lombardi, John L., and David J. Sanchez, "Terrorist Financing and the Tri-Border Area of South America: The Challenge of Effective Governmental Response in a Permissive Environment," in Jeanne K. Giraldo and Harold A. Trinkunas (eds.), *Terrorism Financing and State Responses: A Comparative Perspective*, Stanford, CA: Stanford University Press, 2007.

Madani, Blanca, "Hezbollah's Global Finance Network: The Triple Frontier," *Middle East Intelligence Bulletin*, Vol. 4, No. 1, January 2002. Available at http://www.meib.org/articles/0201_l2.htm (as of September 24, 2008).

"Mafiya: Organized Crime in Russia," *Jane's Intelligence Review—Special Report*, June 1996.

Mak, Lau Fong, *The Sociology of Secret Societies: A Study of Chinese Secret Societies in Singapore and Peninsular Malaysia*, Kuala Lumpur: Oxford University Press, 1981.

Makarenko, Tamara, "A model of terrorist-criminal relations," *Jane's Intelligence Review*, August 2003.

Manwaring, Max G., *Street Gangs: The New Urban Insurgency*, Carlisle, PA: Strategic Studies Institute, U.S. Army War College, March 2005, pp. 8–12. Available at http://www.strategicstudiesinstitute.army.mil/pdffiles/PUB597.pdf (as of September 12, 2008).

Martinez, Ibsen, "Tepito's Way," *The Library of Economics and Liberty*, October 3, 2005. Available at http://www.econlib.org/library/Columns/y2005/MartinezTepito.html (as of October 1, 2008).

McIllwain, Jeffrey Scott, "Intellectual Property Theft and Organized Crime: The Case of Film Piracy," *Trends in Organized Crime*, Vol. 8, No. 4, 2005.

Memorandum submitted by the Police Service of Northern Ireland to the United Kingdom House of Commons Northern Ireland Affairs Select Committee, n.d. Available at http://www.publications.parliament.uk/pa/cm200102/cmselect/cmniaf/978/2011602.htm (as of September 24, 2008).

Milhaupt, Curtis J., and Mark D. West, "The Dark Side of Private Ordering: An Institutional and Empirical Analysis of Organized Crime," *University of Chicago Law Review*, Vol. 67, 2000.

Millar, Kathleen, "Financing Terror: Profits from counterfeit goods pay for attacks," *U.S. Customs Today*, U.S. Customs, Office of Public Affairs, November 2002. Available at http://www.cbp.gov/xp/CustomsToday/2002/November/interpol.xml (as of September 12, 2008).

Motion Picture Association Piracy Loss Estimate Study, 2005, cited in Dan Glickman, "Film Piracy," Interview, C-Span, 201096-1, Washington, D.C. Available at http://www.cspanarchives.org/library/index.php?main_page=product_video_info&products_id=201096-1 (as of September 13,2008).

Motivans, Mark, *Intellectual Property Theft, 2002*, U.S. Department of Justice, Bureau of Justice Statistics, October 2004. Available at http://www.ojp.usdoj.gov/bjs/pub/pdf/ipt02.pdf (as of September 13, 2008).

Myers, Julie, "Testimony by Julie Meyers, Assistant Secretary, U.S. Department of Homeland Security," Customs Budget Authorization, Committee on House Ways and Means Subcommittee on Trade, *LexisNexis Congressional*, July 25, 2006.

Naim, Moises, quoting a 2004 report issued by the Inspector General of the Department of Justice, in *Illicit: How Smugglers, Traffickers and Copycats Are Hijacking the Global Economy*, London: William Heinemann, 2006.

National Criminal Intelligence Service (United Kingdom), *UK Threat Assessment: The Threat from Serious and Organized Crime 2004/5–2005/6*. Available at http://www.ncis.gov.uk/ukta/2004/UKTA_2004-05_2005-06.pdf (as of August 13, 2008).

National Police Agency Japan, "Countermeasures against IPR counterfeiting and piracy," February 2007. Available at www.npa.go.jp/safetylife/seikan36/20070308.pdf (as of July 10, 2008).

Nestares, Carlos Resa, "Transnational Organized Crime Activities in Spain: Structural Factors Explaining Its Penetration," Madrid: University of Madrid, Applied Economics Working Paper, February 27, 2001. Available at http://www.uam.es/personal_pdi/economicas/cresa/text9.html (as of August 13, 2008).

Noble, Ronald K., Interpol, prepared statement. Available at http://www.interpol.int/Public/ICPO/speeches (as of September 12, 2008).

Organisation for Economic Co-operation and Development, *The Economic Impact of Counterfeiting and Piracy: Part IV. Executive Summary*, Directorate for Science, Technology and Industry, Committee on Industry, Innovation and Entrepreneurship, JT03228347, DSTI/IND(2007)9/PART4/REV1, June 4, 2007. Available at http://www.oecd.org/dataoecd/11/38/38704571.pdf (as of September 13, 2008).

"Organized Crime Punishment Law used for first time to target copyright infringers in Japan," Japan and International Motion Picture Copyright Association, press release, July 30, 2007.

Organized Crime Task Force, Police Service of Northern Ireland, *Organized Crime Task Force Annual Report and Threat Assessment*, 2007. Available at http://www.octf.gov.uk (as of September 20, 2008).

————, "New Research on Counterfeiting Looks Towards Consumers," press release, September 28, 2004. Available at http://www.octf.gov.uk/index.cfm/section/News/page/details/key/D03F3464-B0D0-7815-0FEA6E167DAEBD29/?month=9&year=2004 (as of September 28, 2008).

————, *The Threat Assessment 2002: Serious and Organised Crime in Northern Ireland*. Available at http://www.nio.gov.uk/organised_crime_threat_assessment_2002.pdf (as of September 13, 2008).

Peña, Sergio, "Informal Markets: Street Vendors in Mexico City," *Habitat International*, Vol. 23, No. 2, 1999, pp. 363–372.

Picarelli, John T., and Louise Shelly, "The Political Economy of Terrorist Financing," in Jeanne K. Giraldo and Harold A. Trinkunas (eds.), *Terrorism Financing and State Responses: A Comparative Perspective*, Stanford, CA: Stanford University Press, 2007.

Pimental, Stanley, "The Nexus of Organized Crime and Politics in Mexico," *Trends in Organized Crime*, Vol. 4, No. 3, Spring 1999, pp. 9–28.

"Police: Mohammed visited Brazil in 1995," *CNN International*, March 9, 2003. Available at http://edition.cnn.com/2003/WORLD/americas/03/08/mohammed.brazil/index.html (as of September 24, 2008).

Priest, Eric, "The Future of Music and Film Piracy in China," *Berkeley Technology Law Journal*, Vol. 21, No. 2, 2006.

Prober, Joshua, "Accounting for Terror: Debunking the Paradigm of Inexpensive Terrorism," *PolicyWatch/PeaceWatch*, Washington Institute for Near East Policy, PolicyWatch #1041. Available at http://www.washingtoninstitute.org/templateC05.php?CID=2389 (as of September 12, 2008).

Rabasa, Angel, Peter Chalk, Kim Cragin, Sara A. Daly, Heather S. Gregg, Theodore W. Karasik, Kevin A. O'Brien, William Rosenau, *Beyond al-Qaeda: Part 1, The Global Jihadist Movement*, Santa Monica, CA: RAND Corporation, MG-429-AF, 2006. Available at http://www.rand.org/pubs/monographs/MG429/ (as of September 24, 2008).

———, *Beyond al-Qaeda: Part 2, The Outer Rings of the Terrorist Universe*, Santa Monica, CA: RAND Corporation, MG-430-AF, 2006. Available at http://www.rand.org/pubs/monographs/MG430/ (as of September 24, 2008).

Riley, K. Jack, Gregory F. Treverton, Jeremy M. Wilson, and Lois M. Davis, *State and Local Intelligence in the War on Terrorism*, Santa Monica, CA: RAND Corporation, MG-394-RC, 2005. Available at http://www.rand.org/pubs/monographs/MG394/ (as of September 22, 2008).

Roth, Mitchel P., and Murat Sever, "The Kurdish Workers Party (PKK) as Criminal Syndicate: Funding Terrorism through Organized Crime, A Case Study," *Studies in Conflict & Terrorism*, Vol. 30, No. 10, 2007.

Sanderson, Thomas, "Transnational Terror and Organized Crime: Blurring the Lines," *SAIS Review*, Vol. 24, No. 1, 2004.

Sarkar, Sumita, and Arvind Tiwari, "Combating Organised Crime: A Case Study of Mumbai City," *Faultlines*, Vol. 12, 2002. Available at http://www.satp.org/satporgtp/publication/faultlines/volume12/Article5.htm (as of September 24, 2008).

Saviano, Roberto, *Gomorrah: A Personal Journey into the Violent International Empire of Naples' Organized Crime System*, trans. Virginia Jewiss, New York: Farrar, Straus and Giroux, 2007.

Shelley, Louise I., et al., *Methods and Motives: Exploring Links Between Transnational Organized Crime and International Terrorism*, Washington, D.C.: U.S. Department of Justice, Document Number 211207, June 23, 2005. Available at
http://www.ncjrs.gov/pdffiles1/nij/grants/211207.pdf
(as of September 12, 2008).

Silke, Andrew, "In Defense of the Realm: Financing Loyalist Terrorism in Northern Ireland: Part One: Extortion and Blackmail," *Studies in Conflict & Terrorism*, Vol. 21, No. 4, 1998, pp. 331–333.

Siwek, Stephen E., *The True Cost of Motion Picture Piracy to the U.S. Economy*, Institute for Policy Innovation, IPI Center for Technology Freedom, Policy Report 186, 2006, pp. 1–31. Available at
http://www.nbcuni.com/About_NBC_Universal/Intellectual_Property/pdf/Motion_
Picture_Piracy.pdf
(as of September 13, 2008).

Sokolov, Vsevolod, "From Guns to Briefcases: The Evolution of Russian Organized Crime," *World Policy Journal*, Vol. 21, Spring 2004.

Stedman, Lieutenant John C., County of Los Angeles Sheriff's Department, CQ Congressional Testimony, Capitol Hill Hearing Testimony, Committee on Senate Homeland Security and Governmental Affairs, May 25, 2005.

Sutton, Malcolm, *Bear in Mind These Dead: An Index of Deaths from the Conflict in Ireland, 1969–1993*, Belfast: Beyond the Pale Publications, 1994.

UK National Criminal Intelligence Service SU/Drug Project, 2004.

Union de Fabricants, *Counterfeiting and Organised Crime Report*, 3rd ed., Paris, 2005. Available at
http://www.unifab.com/publications/cf_organised_crime_2edition.pdf
(as of September 13, 2008).

————, *Counterfeiting and Organized Crime*, 2003. Available at
http://www.interpol.int/public/financialcrime/intellectualproperty/publications/
udfcounterfeiting.pdf
(as of September 13, 2008).

United Kingdom House of Commons, *The Financing of Terrorism in Northern Ireland: Interim Report on the Proceeds of Crime Bill, HC628,* Northern Ireland Affairs, Fourth Report, n.d. Available at
http://www.publications.parliament.uk/pa/cm200102/cmselect/cmniaf/978/97803.htm
(as of September 23, 2008).

United Nations, *United Nations Convention Against Transnational Organized Crime*, 2000, p. 2. Available at
http://www.uncjin.org/Documents/Conventions/dcatoc/final_documents_2/convention_eng.pdf
(as of September 12, 2008).

United Nations Security Council, *Security Council Al-Qaida, Taliban Sanctions Committee Approves Changes to Consolidated List*, Department of Public Information, July 25, 2006. Available at
http://www.un.org/News/Press/docs/2006/sc8785.doc.htm
(as of September 24, 2008).

————, *First report of the Analytical Support and Sanctions Monitoring Team established pursuant to resolution 1526 (2004) concerning Al-Qaida and the Taliban and associated individuals and entities*, Richard Barrett, Coordinator (S/2004/679), July 31, 2004.

U.S. Department of Justice, "Operation Bell Bottoms Targets Counterfeiting, Narcotics Operation in Los Angeles-Area Clothing Stores," press release, November 6, 2007. Available at
http://losangeles.fbi.gov/dojpressrel/pressrel07/la110607busa.htm
(as of August 1, 2008).

————, "Nineteen Charged with Racketeering to Support Terrorist Organization," press release, March 29, 2006. Available at
http://detroit.fbi.gov/dojpressrel/pressrel06/de032906a.htm
(as of August 1, 2008).

————, Federal Bureau of Investigation, *Report to the National Commission on Terrorist Attacks upon the United States: The FBI's Counterterrorism Program Since September 2001*, submitted April 14, 2004. Available at
http://www.fbi.gov/publications/commission/9-11commissionrep.pdf
(as of August 1, 2008).

————, Office of Justice Programs, Bureau of Justice Statistics, *Drug and Crime Facts, Arrest Seizures,* 2003. Available at
http://www.ojp.usdoj.gov/bjs/dcf/enforce.htm
(as of September 24, 2008).

————, Office of the Inspector General Audit Division, *The Federal Bureau of Investigation's Efforts to Improve the Sharing of Intelligence and Other Information*, Audit Report 04-10, December 2003. Available at
http://www.usdoj.gov/oig/reports/FBI/a0410/final.pdf
(as of August, 1, 2008).

————, Federal Bureau of Investigation, *Terrorism 2000/2001*, FBI Publication 0308. Available at
http://www.fbi.gov/publications/terror/terror2000_2001.htm
(as of September 12, 2008).

U.S. Department of Treasury, "Treasury Targets Hizballah Fundraising Network in the Triple Frontier of Argentina, Brazil, and Paraguay," press release, December 6, 2006. Available at http://paraguay.usembassy.gov/hizballah_fundraising_network_in_the_triple_frontier2.html (as of September 24, 2008).

————, "Treasury Designates Islamic Extremist, Two Companies Supporting Hizballah in Tri-Border Area," press release, June 10, 2004. Available at http://www.treas.gov/press/releases/js1720.htm (as of September 24, 2008).

"U.S. Designates Dawood Ibrahim as Terrorist Support," Washington, D.C.: Office of Public Affairs, United States Department of Treasury, October 16, 2003. Available at http://www.treas.gov/press/releases/js909.htm (as of September 24, 2008).

U.S. General Accounting Office, "Nontraditional Organized Crime: Law Enforcement Officials' Perspectives on Five Criminal Groups," Report number OSI-18-19, 1989. Available at http://archive.gao.gov/d26t7/139919.pdf (as of September 24, 2008).

Vicziany, Marika, "Understanding the 1993 Mumbai Bombings: Madrassas and the Hierarchy of Terror," *South Asia: Journal of South Asian Studies*, Vol. 30, No. 1, April 2007, pp. 43–73.

Willan, Philip, "Camorra factions vie for control of Naples drugs market," *Jane's Intelligence Review*, February 1, 2005.

————, "Police crack down on Camorra's counterfeit goods trade," *Jane's Intelligence Review*, March 7, 2005.

Williams, Phil, "Terrorist Financing and Organized Crime: Nexus, Appropriation or Transformation?" in Thomas J. Biersteker and Sue E. Eckert (eds.), *Countering the Financing of Terrorism*, London: Routledge, 2007.

————, *Organized Crime and Terrorism*, Washington, D.C.: Defense Intelligence Agency, Project on Terrorist Financing 2004–2005, 2005.

Wilson, Gary I., and John P. Sullivan, *On Gangs, Crime, and Terrorism,* Special to Defense and the National Interest, February 28, 2007. Available at http://www.d-n-i.net/fcs/pdf/wilson_sullivan_gangs_terrorism.pdf (as of September 12, 2008).

Wilson, John, *Karachi, a Terror Capital in the Making*, New Delhi: Rupa & Co., in association with Observer Research Foundation, 2003.

Yar, Majid, "The Global 'Epidemic' of Movie 'Piracy': Crime-Wave or Social Construction?" *Media, Culture & Society*, Vol. 27, No. 5, 2005, p. 680.

Zaidi, S. Hussain, *Black Friday: The True Story of the Bombay Bomb Blasts*, New Delhi and New York: Penguin Books, 2002, p. 25.

Zhang, Sheldon, *Chinese Human Smuggling Organizations: Families, Social Networks, and Cultural Imperatives*, Stanford, CA: Stanford University Press, 2008.